Just say
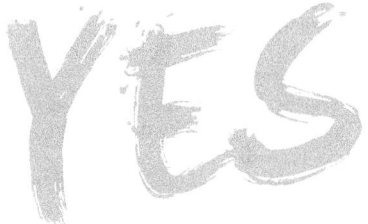

**YOU CAN TRUST GOD
IN YOUR JOURNEY**

Deborah Hilton

Just say YES
Copyright © Deborah Hilton, 2016

Published by Deborah Hilton
Email: deborahannehilton@gmail.com
Facebook Page: https://www.facebook.com/IsayYES/

All rights reserved. No part of this publication may be reproduced, stored in or introduced into a database and retrieval system or transmitted in any form or any means (electronic, mechanical, photocopying, recording or otherwise) without the prior written permission of the publisher.

All Scripture quotations, unless otherwise indicated, are taken from the Holy Bible, New International Version®, NIV®. Copyright ©1973, 1978, 1984, 2011 by Biblica, Inc.™ Used by permission of Zondervan. All rights reserved.
Scripture quotations marked (NLT) are taken from the Holy Bible, New Living Translation, copyright ©1996, 2004, 2007, 2013, 2015 by Tyndale House Foundation. Used by permission of Tyndale House Publishers, Inc., Carol Stream, Illinois 60188. All rights reserved.
Scripture quotations marked (TLB) are taken from The Living Bible copyright © 1971. Used by permission of Tyndale House Publishers, Inc., Carol Stream, Illinois 60188. All rights reserved.
Scripture quotations marked (NKJV) are taken from the New King James Version. Copyright © 1982 by Thomas Nelson, Inc. Used by permission. All rights reserved.
Scripture quotations marked (AMP) are taken from the Amplified® Bible, Copyright © 1954, 1958, 1962, 1964, 1965, 1987 by The Lockman Foundation Used by permission.
Scripture quotations marked (NASB) are taken from the New American Standard Bible®, Copyright © 1960, 1962, 1963, 1968, 1971, 1972, 1973, 1975, 1977, 1995 by The Lockman Foundation Used by permission.
Scripture quotations marked (ISV) are taken from the Holy Bible: International Standard Version®. Copyright © 1996-forever by The ISV Foundation. All rights reserved internationally. Used by permission.
Scripture quotations marked (CEV) are taken from the Contemporary English Version Copyright © 1991, 1992, 1995 by American Bible Society. Used by Permission.
Scripture quotations marked (GNT) are taken from the Good News Translation in Today's English Version- Second Edition Copyright © 1992 by American Bible Society. Used by Permission.
Scripture quotations marked (ESV) are taken from the ESV® Bible (The Holy Bible, English Standard Version®), copyright © 2001 by Crossway, a publishing ministry of Good News Publishers. Used by permission. All rights reserved.
Scripture quotations from THE MESSAGE. Copyright © by Eugene H. Peterson 1993, 1994, 1995, 1996, 2000, 2001, 2002. Used by permission of NavPress. All rights reserved. Represented by Tyndale House Publishers, Inc.

National Library of Australia Cataloguing-in-Publication entry:
Hilton, Deborah Anne, 2016 – author.
Just say YES: you can trust God in your journey/Deborah Hilton

ISBN: 978-0-9946362-0-1 (paperback)
Self-publishing --Australia--

Design by Cherie Mountney.
Photo of Deborah Hilton by AOG World Relief

Printed and bound in Australia, United States or United Kingdom
by IngramSpark, Lightning Source Inc.

My deep appreciation to...

PAUL

My amazing husband for walking this journey of writing with me, allowing me space and time to write. You always encourage me in whatever I do. Thanks for believing in me and cheering me on as I have shared each day's entries with you for your comments and feedback. I am blessed to have you as my partner, my anchor and my helpmate, in life. I love you.

BELINDA AND JOSH

For being the best children a mum could ask for. You encouraged me with your words, "We are proud of you mum" every time I talked about this book. Thank you both.

AOG WORLD RELIEF

My team in Vietnam, who gave me the time and space to write. I am blessed to do life with such amazing people.

TO THE MANY

Those faithful friends who often connected with me over this book-writing season, to ask me: "How are you going with your book?" "Keep going Deb, this is a God thing for His purposes." "You have to do this, Deb!" To all of you I want to say that you have no idea how much your applauding me has spurred me on, when at times I thought, "Really God! You want me to write this, there are so many great authors out there." It was during those times God would remind me by a whisper or by people like you, that I was truly doing this for the Master's service. I am blessed beyond measure to have people like you in my life.

COREY TURNER

A thank you goes out to you for articulating in just a few words, the essence of my book's message when you said, "I see the book's title called 'Just say YES'", and even though you were not telling me I should call it that, the moment you spoke it out, not only did those words go straight into my spirit, but I saw crystal clear, exactly what the front cover looked like. This was a prophetic moment. So here it is Corey, in print!

JILLIAN BRADY AND GORDON (GUS) YEARSLEY

Thank you for spending numerous hours poring over these pages with your editing eyes, fine tuning the little things that make the difference.

CHERIE MOUNTNEY

Thank you for working with me on creating the right look for this book, being patient with me as we batted back and forth to get it just right.

THE HOLY SPIRIT

On the day I opened up my computer to begin the journey of writing this book, You and I made a deal. I said to You that day, and every day I wrote, "Well, God the Father wants me to write this, Holy Spirit, so I will write, but I need You to speak. I cannot do this unless You give me the words to say. You wrote this book, these are Your writings, and I give You all the glory." Thank you Holy Spirit, my God whisperer, for being faithful all the way.

What others are saying about 'Just Say *Yes*'

Deb Hilton and her husband Paul are respected leaders who have served the Lord with distinction for many years in the challenging context of Vietnam. They are celebrated broadly by their sending movement, the Australian Christian Churches, because of their faithfulness to the call, and their effectiveness on the field. We are honoured to be their friends.

In her book 'Just Say YES', Deb takes us on a journey of the heart. She reminds us that obedience unlocks miracles. Accept her invitation to take your own personal journey of faith, and discover the wonder of God's love and the adventure that awaits everyone that says "Yes" to Him.

WAYNE AND LYN ALCORN
Senior Pastors Hope Centre (Brisbane Australia)
National President Australian Christian Churches (ACC)

Deb takes us on an amazing journey of faith and personal growth. As we journey with her we are inspired, challenged and with her, we grow in faith. Deb's openness challenges us to see our own challenges in a new light and realize that we all experience obstacles on our faith journey but we can overcome them and live a life of significance. I have known Deb and her husband Paul for many years, and I have watched them grow through many of these experiences into people of greater passion and fruitfulness in ministry. Deb is an inspiration. I know you will be blessed by this book and her story.

ALUN DAVIES
Director Australian Christian Churches
International (ACCI)
Vice-President Australian Christian Churches (ACC)

"Yes"! Possibly the most powerful word. I do know that it is also the most dangerous word. It is a word that will need all your courage and faith. It will change your life—"Yes". My friend Deborah Hilton will take you on her "Yes" journey and her faith-fueled story will show you all the implications of "Yes". This real and transparent book will encourage your "Yes" and propel you into your God-ordained destiny!

SAM CHAND
Leadership Consultant
Author of 'Leadership Pain'

Deb and Paul Hilton are outstanding leaders working in a culturally diverse and rewarding region of the world. Deb is an exceptional author and her book 'Just say YES' is an inspiring chronicle of her journey in Vietnam. Her book is filled with stirring stories and powerful principles for success. Vietnam will never be the same because of them! Hundreds of thousands of people will forever be impacted by them. Their work, their life, their spirit and their passion will live on for generations. This book is testament to their legacy. It was a great read and I recommend it!

TOM RAWLS
Senior Pastor of Proclaimers
A 21st Century church Norwich, England

DON'T READ THIS BOOK if you don't want to be challenged, have fresh faith stir you to action, and be motivated to get up do all you can to fulfil your God-given destiny and so change your world. Deb and Paul's story is a testimony to the truth that if your life is boring, predictable and disappointing… you didn't get there by following Jesus! Read this book, then get down on your knees and just say, "YES" to Jesus.

SEAN STANTON
Senior Pastor Life Unlimited Church
National Secretary Australian Christian Churches (ACC)

God wants to touch the world. As humans, we are His hands and feet, but so often we discredit ourselves and are sure that "someone else" must be doing that work. Deborah Hilton is a General in the global world of missions. She's a woman that said "Yes" to the call and is now literally being the hands and feet of Jesus across the globe. I'm excited that her experience, knowledge and wisdom are being put down on paper, which I know will inspire and encourage others to listen to that small voice inside and say "Yes" to the great plan that God has for them.

KARYN EY
State Executive Member Australian Christian Churches (ACC) South Australia
Global Missions Pastor Influencers Church

'Just Say YES' is a clear and compelling call to live by faith and follow God's call on your life. Deborah's book is choc-a-block full of inspiring stories and insights that will take your faith deeper and encourage you to say "Yes" to God no matter your history or background. Deborah has been used by God to impact nations across the globe and this book shows you how you can do the same.

COREY TURNER
International speaker, author and pastor
Founder of Corey Turner Ministries Inc

In this book the word "Yes" almost takes on a powerful new meaning. Deb uses it as a word that brings along with it the full realisation of joy combined with sacrifice, fulfilment combined with hard work, and the understanding of a "calling". That calling beckoned and resonated with her as she continued on the journey to seeing a dream fulfilled. Because of this, she is so qualified, through all that she describes in her story after story and situation after situation in the book, to talk about the battle to walk into destiny.

Deb does this with an open and honest conversational style that will draw you into her heart and keep you cheering Deb and her family until the final goal is achieved… and you understand the significance of this: "Don't be another statistic, another person who at the end of their life says: "I wish I had", but be the one who says: "I'm glad I did".

Enjoy! I did!

VALERY MURPHY
Leaderscape

'Just Say YES' is an insightful and compelling account of how our obedience unlocks heaven's power and propels us into our divine purpose. It was a conversation with Deb a few years ago that caused me to take God at His word and shifted me from doubtful hesitation to a steadfast "Yes". Those same threads of encouragement and faith are woven through the pages of this book. Deb's experience and wisdom and her personable and engaging style mean this book is a valuable and easy read for anyone.

JANINE KUBALA
Director Kubala Ministries
Founder of Esther's Voice

CONTENTS

FOREWORD

INTRODUCTION

PART 1 | My Story

1. Your past should not define your future
2. Set and match
3. Our first 'Just say YES' moment

PART 2 | The Tassie Experience

4. Why Tasmania?
5. Tough times ahead
6. Breaking out of the shell
7. What is Missions anyway?
8. That first trip
9. Leaving things in our hands
10. More than enough
11. Here we go!
12. The issue of doubt and fear

PART 3 | 200 Days of Miracles

DON'T SKIP THE EPILOGUE

NOTES

FOREWORD

There are many books out there saying, "Go for it. Go after your call." So why am I writing another one? The answer is simple; I believe we all have a story for the world to glean from and from my perspective, I want the world to know that if I can do it, you can too.

The question I asked myself at the start of this mammoth undertaking of writing was, "Where do I begin? What is the launching pad for telling my story?" I wanted to pour out the message deep within my heart that I am burdened with, and bursting to tell everyone: the revelation of truth that YES you can trust God in your journey of life. When you truly grasp this biblical reality and run with it, by simply saying YES to God with abandoned faith, you will discover that living your destined, purposed-filled life is not only possible but it will be a certainty!

> You can live beyond your safe zone to fulfill the call that God has for your life and still stay intact, I promise!

God simply said to me, "Just start writing, and I will fill the pages."

God's mandate to me: "Write a book. Tell your story so others will be encouraged and inspired, knowing it doesn't take a superman or woman to fulfill all the dreams and purposes that I have put inside all my people. That it only takes believing in Me and who I am in them and moving forward from that position."

My personal drive: To write a book that shouted out loud to everyone this message,
> "Guess what, you do have a call of God on your life, yes you. You are not exempt and the world needs you and if you just step out, God will prove He can be trusted every step of the way."

I know what you are thinking: "I'm good right here". Some of you haven't done anything yet because you have convinced yourself it is safer to do nothing rather than something that might not work out even though you don't feel fulfilled. You may not be verbalising it, but inside you feel that the security of the mundane is a less scary path than the unknown.

I can tell you now from my personal experience, you can live beyond your safe zone to fulfill the call that God has for your life and still stay intact, I promise!

He will be with you, provide for you, turn up and work it out for you. He is just waiting for you to say YES. Come on, you know you are not satisfied where you are, so it's time to step up to the plate. Stand up, move forward and don't look back.

INTRODUCTION

There have been a number of surveys taken with people in the last stages of their life, whether that be related to age or illness, asking this one question, "If you had the opportunity to do life again, what would you do differently?" One of these very surveys was referred to in a podcast I listened to by Dr. Tony Campolo, Professor of Sociology, Eastern College, St. David's, Pennsylvania. This survey was taken with 50 people aged 95 years and older and the results are noteworthy. The top three answers from the survey were as follows:

1. Reflect more.

These seniors said they would have taken the time to think about what was going on around them and live their lives along well thought-out priorities. They would have contemplated the meaning of life, family and work much more.

2. Risk more.

These wonderful aged human beings said they would have taken more chances in life. If they could relive their lives over again, they wouldn't have been so scared to take risks. They would have developed more courage to venture out of their comfort zones.

3. Do things that would outlast them.

They wanted to know that their lives counted for something, that long after they left this world, somehow their impact would live on.

These results are a wake up call to many of us. Let's not get to the end of our lives and be surveyed with answers of "I wish!"

Right now, whatever age you are, if you continue to breathe air on this earth, you still have the opportunity to take advice from these elderly people by choosing to stand up and make a decision that from this day forward, you will, at the end of your life, leave completely emptied out and satisfied rather than being full of regret with that potential still sitting inside of you.

Potential is what we are capable of becoming in every area of our life. Our potential is boundless. The only thing that can limit us from becoming all that we can be, is us.

The sad truth is, that throughout history, most potential has simply been buried in multitudes of cemeteries. Stories untold, songs unsung, journeys never taken, businesses never started, ministries never born, vision uncast and people never connected.

Why is this? What stops us from fulfilling our potential? I don't think it is from a lack of wanting to do all the things that are in our heart, because each one of us has dreams, or at least thoughts of dreams, throughout our lives. So why is it that so many don't move beyond the thought stage?

I believe the answer lies in the 'parable of the soil' found in Luke 8:5-8. Here is that parable according to Deb Hilton.

The Path: You know what you should do but you don't do it because it's easier just to keep going the way you are. "I'm not really satisfied with my life but I am comfortable and it's safe where I'm at."

The Rocky Soil: You know what you should do and you think it is a great idea. You even begin to put your dream into motion, but after a while you give up because it's just too much hard work to change or keep the momentum going, so you go back to how you were.

The Weedy Soil: You change and start putting good things in your soil; you are on a roll, but then after a while, you start to worry about everything. Is it all going to work out the way you want? Worries start to rob you of all the good things you have put into your soil. You allow them to become the main thing in your world instead of trusting God to bless all the good things you have put in. So eventually you go back to how you were.

The Good Soil: You know what you should do, so you begin to change and put good things into your soil, and know that if you keep going, and don't give up, you will achieve your dream, your purpose, your vision. Even when things get rocky, you continue to stay motivated because you believe that if you keep going, you will succeed. You fill your life with things that will do you good, things that will help you grow, to strengthen and stretch you to keep you on the path to your goal. Sometimes things don't go according to your expectations, but still, you stay on the path, planted in the soil because you know it's worth it. In time you start to see the seeds grow and produce fruit, lots of fruit, and before you know it, you are living that dream, that vision, the very purpose you were put on this earth to do. Now you are dancing.

It is so easy to make excuses. For example, you say, "I'm not smart enough or positioned well enough to make anything happen. You don't understand where I came from, what my life has been like." Well I say take a moment to research people who have been successful in life and you will find many of them were either kicked out of school or told they wouldn't become anything in life, yet today, they are living their dream.

Talk to successful writers, people in film and on stage, men and women who have built successful businesses, or people who are influencing the world through preaching, teaching or training. Talk to those who are now being a voice for defenseless lives, seeing others lifted from their destitution. Their stories are more often than not, your story, my story. Some of these people began in broken homes, were homeless, abused, brought up in poverty, even born with handicaps but they didn't let that define what their future would look like.

What is the difference between those who do and those who don't? What is the mark of those living out their purpose and those who aren't? The difference is right in front of you. It's you. It starts with you.

> Don't be another statistic, another person, who at the end of their life says, "I wish I had," but be one who says, "I'm glad I did." The world needs more "I'm glad I did people."

We must change our "I can't" to "I can, I'm called, I'm destined, I'm purposed to live a life beyond where I am now." The process is simple. First we must choose! Choose to stand up from where we are now and take one step forward. Every successful person begins with those two ingredients: choosing, and moving. So are you ready? I challenge you right at the start of this journey with me to get up now and take that first step. If you do just that, you will find the yoke of 'impossible' falls off you and the steps ahead of you become easier to walk. The first step is always the hardest, so if you have chosen to do that, well done!

Then as you choose to continue putting one step in front of the other, one day you look behind you and to your own surprise, find how far you have come and how close you are, to seeing your purposed call being fulfilled for your life.

PART 1: My Story

1
YOUR PAST SHOULD NOT DEFINE YOUR FUTURE

I was brought up in a dysfunctional home with a mentally ill father who was in and out of psychiatric hospitals all his married life. This meant my mother had to be a both mother and father to her three children and in those days it was not common to be in a single parent family. This made us the odd ones out in our neighbourhood.

Being a paranoid schizophrenic, my father often didn't realise what he was doing, which meant one minute, he would be irrational and the next seemingly normal. As I walked home from school each day, my thoughts would turn to my mother. How I would find her? Would I come home to my father hitting or kissing her today? In his good times, you could have a conversation with him. It wasn't completely normal, but he could communicate with you. During those times I wanted to get close to him, to understand him, know how he thought, and I desperately wanted him to be like my friends' fathers who played games with them and took them on outings, but for my father, this was not possible because even the simplest of activities was not something he was capable of, therefore those dreams of normal family life remained a fantasy in my mind. At his worst, he would become dangerously violent and during those times, he would be sent back to hospital for yet another stint where shock treatment was administered to settle him down. For days after the electricity had been sent through my father's brain, he would become almost zombie like. Shock treatment is a terrible thing.

During the times my father was at home, it was very difficult to concentrate at school knowing that at the end of my day I would have to return to a very tense atmosphere. When it was just Mum, my brother, sister and I at home, there was peace! My mother truly is one of my heroes because she continued to give her best during these trying times, doing all she could to make home for us, a sanctuary rather than a battlefield.

Because of the situation in our home, I didn't do well at school and because I didn't do well at school I thought I was not smart.

Isn't it interesting how circumstances in our lives can lead us to wrong perceptions of who we truly are! I believe many people are not doing what they are meant to do in life simply because of this belief.

Because my father was living between hospital and home, it was not easy for my mother to get a pension. This meant often times we were left with no money to live on. Eventually she was granted a part pension but it hardly covered our living expenses and sometimes she would have to choose between paying the electricity bill and feeding us. Being the good mother she was, she would always choose to feed us over having lighting and heating. We were blessed with great neighbours who looked out for us and from time to time, came to the rescue by helping out with the electricity and other bills.

Christmas time was especially difficult for our mother because she would want to give us gifts like all the other children in the neighbourhood. I don't know how she did it, but somehow she would manage to put aside a small amount throughout the year so she could buy each of us a few small gifts. Wrapping them ever so lovingly, she would put them under the tree and wait for morning to come so she could enjoy the excitement on our faces that said, "Yes, Santa came to our place too!" We would tear off the paper in seconds just like every other child does when receiving a gift and lift up our prized treasures for her and each other to see. Although the gifts were small, we were happy and thankful to our mum for making Christmas special.

On a few occasions we had an added bonus at Christmas, when the local Catholic Church would bring us a parcel of food and gifts. Every year this church would prepare parcels for the poor in their local area and we were one of the families on their list. To us it was exciting because receiving extra gifts and extra food was a huge treat and for our mother, an enormous blessing; however, it was also a reminder that we were the poor family in our particular neighbourhood.

Although we were poor, and our father was in and out of our home in his unstable condition, our mother made us feel secure and did everything in her power to make life normal for us even though it was anything but normal for her.

I remember that each time our father was sent back to hospital, the psychiatrist demanded that our mother go to Sydney to meet with him. She would have to go every second weekend and not only did she have to meet with him, but the psychiatrist would insist she stay in the hospital for the weekend (in the same ward with the mentally ill patients) and if she didn't do that he would release my father to come home even in his unstable condition. This was not a pleasant experience for her but she did it to protect us, her family.

To understand the dynamics of my father being home in his unstable condition, you have to know it forced us to be on guard constantly. Our mother and us three children would need to watch our words and actions at all times for fear of my father snapping, and when he did, he would get very angry and it was our mother would feel the brunt of that anger. One time we came home from school to find her in tears and packing our bags saying, we have to get out of here. Although she didn't say what went on that day, it was obvious he had abused her once again.

Another time we came home from school to find her quite subdued. The day's events brought with it a close encounter with death as my father had picked up one of her steel healed stiletto shoes and came for her. She cried out to the Lord saying, "Jesus, please stop him." Immediately, he dropped the shoe and sat down. Thankfully God stepped in, as I hate to think how we would have found our mother when we arrived home that day. Although we three children were not the target of his physical abuse, we certainly were emotionally.

Although our neighbours and the local Protestant and Catholic churches were kind to us, school was not. Everyone knew we were the poor family in the school and were often ridiculed. For me, ridicule was daily and for my brother, he was often beaten up. I remember one time my mother had to come to the school to talk about our situation and how we were being treated. The principal tried to help, but to no avail.

You can imagine our self-esteem was not what you would call a healthy one. For me, the last day of school was the best day of school. I couldn't wait to get out of there. I no longer trusted kids my age. I believed no one of my age group liked or accepted me. Because of the way I was treated at school, I put up a wall called suspicion and anyone reaching out to me was forced through that filter.

Not long after my final year at school we moved churches. Our old church was nice and filled with lovely old people. I trusted old people, but on entering the doorway of our new church home for the first time, I was overwhelmed by just how many young people there were. We'd no sooner sat down when some of the girls were introducing themselves to me and asking me to sit with them. Of course I declined. I was not going down that path again. But week after week, these bubbly, smiling faces would rock up to ask me to join them. Not wanting to appear impolite, I eventually agreed. As they chatted away, they would pull me into their conversation, asking me about myself. They seemed so friendly, but still wearing a cloak of suspicion, I waited for them to turn on me. It never happened. Could they actually like me? I began to see something in them that was definitely not in any of my old school 'friends.' Genuine love and friendship! These two ingredients started to penetrate my protected spirit. It took a long time for me to trust them, and I am grateful for their patience. I began opening my heart to let them in, and little by little, a process of healing began. God definitely used these particular girls, girls of my own age, who forged a new-found trust in me.

I wanted to tell you my story because so many people use circumstances of the past to excuse them from doing what they know they should do with their life today. All of us have a story. All of us have circumstances that we wish were different in our life. The truth is, we live in a broken and imperfect world, but that doesn't mean we have to live a broken life.

Lizzie Velasquez, another one of my heroes truly depicts what it means to live beyond difficult circumstances. Lizzie was born with a rare congenital disease, which among other symptoms, prevents her from storing body fat. Due to this condition, she was bullied during her childhood and early youth, and even found herself on a YouTube clip titled 'The Ugliest Woman', viewed by more than four million people who added their own hurtful comments under the video. Initially hurt by such cruelty, she made a decision. Her words: "Am I going to let those comments define me, or I am going to turn it around and use those comments as a ladder to climb up to my goals, use them to motivate me and light my fire to achieve my goals."

Today Lizzie is, among other things, a well-known motivational speaker and activist against bullying.

What Lizzie is actually saying is also stated in James 1:2-4 (NIV)

> Consider it pure joy, my brothers and sisters, whenever you face trials of many kinds, because you know that the testing of your faith produces perseverance. Let perseverance finish its work so that you may be mature and complete, not lacking anything.

This is not saying, "Yay, I have this difficulty." What it is saying is, let the difficulty forge something in you, a platform to build on. Our circumstances can actually enhance our life and add to who we are and it can give us strength!

2
SET AND MATCH

I had been going to our new church for almost six months when, one Sunday morning, three cool guys walked in for the first time. There weren't a lot of young guys in our church so when these three walked in, all us girls sat up and took notice, with thoughts running through our minds, "There's not just one, but three of them!" Yay for us girls!

I don't know why, but the guys in the church didn't seem so star-struck! For me, I had already met these guys at a recent youth camp through a mutual friend but just briefly. When they walked in to church that day, I said with a little attitude in my voice, "Oh, I already know these guys." Slight exaggeration but hey, I was sixteen. You remember being sixteen right! Maybe you are sixteen now, so you get what I am saying. Needless to say, I felt confident enough to go up to chat with them. Well actually, I took my brother up with me for backup but before I knew it, all the youth were surrounding these three musketeers, welcoming them and making them feel at home! I loved that about our little church.

Being a small church though, there weren't a lot of young people. In fact we could easily fit into two cars when going out together. Now, you are thinking, "Oh so, you only had about eight to ten people in your youth group?" Ah, no! Think of how many people you can squeeze into a car, a station wagon actually, without falling out and times it by two. Now count! Yes, that is how we rolled in those days, but we seemed to get away with it. I always seemed to end up in brother number two's car, Paul's car, but would always clamber into the very back, the no seats section with the crowds because it was the dare zone. Even back then, when there were no seatbelt rules, it was not legal to sit in the back section of a station wagon car so if we saw the police coming our way, we would have to quickly duck our heads until they passed by. (I don't recommend you to follow my lead on this one). We were all just friends and enjoyed doing everything together. We loved God, loved each other and loved adventure even though some of our escapades were a little crazy.

It wasn't long though before Paul and I began to notice each other beyond friendship, but neither of us would admit what was happening between us. Our friends on the other hand, were quite aware that we were fond of each other and were not going to sit back and wait until we got our act together, so they arranged for us to be alone at a friend's upcoming birthday party. One minute we were all in the party room together and the next, everyone had disappeared, leaving Paul and I alone. We had no idea at first what was going on, but soon figured it out. Now it was awkward, for me at least! But Paul in his valiant way, came and sat with me, told me how much he liked me and asked if I would like to be his girlfriend.

As I was about to answer, we heard noises and looked up to see all our friends' grinning faces squashed against the windows peering in. To say that this romantic pivotal moment for us was not the quiet, private one we had anticipated is an understatement, as all our friends began cheering from the sideline. It was ok though, we were happy to share our new found love with the people who meant the most to us, our amazing friends who were journeying with us through our youth years.

I was sixteen when I began to date Paul and by the time I was eighteen, we were engaged. It was obvious that God had led us both to that little church we attended in our early days of courtship and where we stayed until just after we got married.

We married when I was at the tender age of nineteen and within a few years had two beautiful children, Belinda and Josh. Life was complete.

I am blessed beyond measure, to have such an amazing man by my side. Throughout our life together, Paul has been, and continues to be, my greatest fan. He always believes in me and wants to bring out the best in me. He is my anchor, my friend, my husband; a real gift from God.

3
OUR FIRST 'JUST SAY YES' MOMENT

We had just sat down on our lounge after a full day of moving house feeling very satisfied that we were finally in our newly built dream home. After many years of working hard, saving and sacrificing, we were in! We were so happy and looked forward to the years of memories that we were going to make, to treasure in the future.

As we sat down on the lounge that day, my husband Paul, announced to our friends who were still at the house, "Well, if God took all this away tomorrow, it wouldn't matter because He would have something else for us." The moment that rolled out of his mouth I was floored. I could not believe what he had just said. Not because I didn't believe in his statement, but the fact he said that! Why? Just one week preceding our move into this luxurious place, that I had anxiously been waiting to get into, God spoke to me and said, "If I ask you to give this house up, will you do it?"

At first, I thought, this can't possibly be God. Where was this thought coming from? It had to be the enemy trying to rob me of my joy. I questioned myself on whether this was just my own fear thoughts, but God's question to me kept ringing in my ears daily. It became all consuming. For that entire week I struggled with that thought, but the more I wrestled with it, the more I knew in my spirit that this in fact was God speaking, asking me, "Deb, are you willing to give up this place if I ask you to?"

During that week, I asked myself if I was willing to give up the place that we had just poured months into building and two years into planning. This place that we had dreamed of and would celebrate numerous birthdays and Christmases in. A place that we had purposed to be a haven for people to come stay, and be blessed in. The week was coming to an end and I knew I had to come up with an answer before we moved in and within a day of moving, I settled in my spirit, that it was OK and said to the Lord, "Ok God, if you ask me to give it up, I will do it." I did not tell Paul about this challenge God had put before me because for one, I thought it was just to test my own faith and secondly, I didn't want Paul getting any ideas about building again! Yet here he was, the day we move in, announcing this same conviction that God had put in my heart.

Well, that dream home which we enjoyed, opened to many visitors and did ministry in, was ours for just three short years before God did ask us to give it up and move. Not just move house, but move interstate.

In the natural it seemed crazy. We were comfortable, we were doing ministry in the local church, Paul had a great job, our kids Belinda and Josh were happy at their school and we had the best friends anyone could ask for. All was well with our world.

However God had spoken to us three years earlier when we had moved into our house, and we had settled it in our hearts that our default answer would be YES if and when the time came. It was not a difficult decision because God had already prepared our hearts. We had made a commitment to Him, "Yes Lord, if you ask us to give it up we will do it." Now He was handing out that spiritual agreement to us to see if we would willingly put our 'yes' stamp on it as we had promised.

If we had said no to God, He would have still loved us just the same, because we serve a God of grace. He will not demand that we stick to our agreement even when we have signed the papers, but He desires so much, the best for us, so He gently keeps speaking to our hearts by His Spirit saying, "For I know the plans I have for you," declares the Lord, "plans to prosper you, plans to give you hope and a future." Jeremiah 29:11 (NIV) Trust me! Yes, God is a God of second and third chances, but obeying on that first count saves us a lot of going around the mountain many times. I am so glad we made the choice to honour our agreement with God on the first count.

After we had announced our plans to everyone, not all greeted us with cheers and delight. In some cases it was just the opposite. "This is a crazy move." "I can't see this is actually a God thing, are you sure about this?" "Why would you do that, you have everything going great for you right here and how can you give up this beautiful house?" Then there was our extended family, who found the whole idea difficult to understand. "Why would you up and leave us? Can't you serve God here?" I'm so glad God spoke to us three years earlier, which was an anchor for us to push through and move forward.

It is so important to know when something is a God idea as opposed to a good idea. A God idea needs to settle in your spirit because the best intentioned people will try and convince you otherwise.

> It is so important to know when something is a God idea as opposed to a good idea.

Part 2: The Tassie Experience

4
WHY TASMANIA?

Good question. Glad you asked!

Our version and the short answer is this; it came about by Paul deciding to fall down and break his ankle in several places, it taking a long time to heal and all the while continuing to work his butt off (Can I say that? Oh well, I just did,) to keep us in the style we were accustomed, then needing to take a much deserved holiday, and Tasmania was our preferred destination. That was our version.

God's version was a little bit more predestined. OK, Paul has broken his ankle, he chooses to still work like a dog. They will take a holiday after this, so I will put Tasmania in their hearts as a preferred choice because Tasmania has been in My mind's eye for them since I asked them to move three years ago.

After returning from that holiday, Tasmania would not leave us. It wasn't just the usual, wow, what a nice place, I could live there feeling.

A shift had happened in our hearts. We couldn't put our finger on it except we sensed, change was coming to us. Then over the following weeks everywhere we looked Tasmania came up. Cars with Tasmanian number plates seemed like they were everywhere we went which was not something we had seen before in Newcastle. The Morning Show on television decided to televise their show from Tasmania all the following week. We would meet people who for some reason would begin talking about Tasmania and how beautiful it was. We couldn't escape it. If we weren't getting the message then, we never would.

We had to investigate! We were particularly drawn to Hobart, the capital, so Paul went back down to Tasmania to meet with pastors of the local churches to hear their hearts for their church and the state. Paul was particularly interested in meeting the pastors who had just planted a new church and during that meeting, as they shared their vision they also mentioned that they were praying for a couple to come and work with them to support them in their venture. At that moment, hearts connected.

This was for us.

And so our journey begins…

It was the 13th December, 1991 when we landed on Tasmanian soil. We were excited because everything was new and we felt like we were on an adventure! This was going to be great because we had followed the call of God and everything was falling into place! We found a house to rent, a business to run and schools for the kids. It was going to be a fantastic ride!

The call from God to Tasmania was very clear. We were to support a couple who had just planted a church and help them in any way we could to build this church. We also had to have employment to support us, so because Paul had always been in business, he found a business that we felt was right for him, so he bought it.

At first, things were wonderful, just enjoying the newness of this beautiful place. Every day we ventured out to discover yet something else new and unfamiliar. It felt like a big long holiday.

Our first Sunday in church gave us a real sense of fulfillment in our hearts because we were right in the centre of God's will. The church was new, it was fresh and everyone was enthusiastic to see it grow.

Being a new church, there were lots of firsts. One first, was to have a church family camp. I began to ponder on what a beautiful and powerful time this would be. A place where there would be no interruptions, everyone together, bonding as a church and having an amazing corporate time with God. Nestled in the beautiful bush setting of Orana Camp Grounds on Roches Beach near Hobart, the setting would be perfect. This was going to be a great time for us all!

As we gathered together for our first meeting in the big cement brick hall, everyone was full of expectancy. We could sense the presence of the Holy Spirit right from the beginning. Being part of the music team, it was a privilege for me to be leading everyone into worship. As we struck that first note, it was like heaven came down and filled every corner, it couldn't get better than this.

We had invited a guest speaker to come for our meetings and we were all looking forward to having such a great man of God share at this, our very first family gathering. I would love to say that I remember so well what he spoke on in that first meeting, but I can't. Yet, it was to become one of the most defining moments in our journey ahead. As he finished his message to the church he asked people to come forward for prayer.

We were very enthusiastic to get all that God had for us in this new season, so we didn't waste any time getting to the front to be prayed for. We had not been standing there long, when this guest preacher looked straight at Paul and me and said, "I have a word for you!" My heart jumped. I thought "This is going to be so good, bring it on." I was so sure it would be something like, "good and faithful servants, leaving your homeland and coming to a place you don't know to serve me." Or, "I have got some amazing stuff in store for you guys down here. Are you ready for it?" My anticipation grew as our guest speaker looked us straight in the eye and said, "God has called you to this place." Immediately I began to get excited. "Yes, more confirmation right at the beginning. That's what we need." Then he continued by saying, "Don't look to the left or to the right but straight ahead at what God has called you here for." At this point, my mind is running alongside him and as he is speaking. I am thinking, "Yes, of course, we want to do that, we can do that. That is why we are here, we don't want to be distracted, we want to stay focused. We don't want to be looking left or right, but aim at the target God has for us here." And while I am enjoying those moments of wonderful confirmation, this lovely pastor pulled out his gun and shot us. Well, not literally, but what he said next were words that were totally unexpected and hit us hard. Words that we didn't want to hear. What he said next caused our eyes to open as he directed these words into our hearts, "Stay focused because there are tough times ahead, you are in for tough times." As I began to process those words, I thought to myself, "Really? Tough times? We were not expecting that little tag at the end. Tough times ahead! Really God? Isn't everything supposed to go smoothly when you are in God's will? Don't blessings follow obedience?" But after the initial shock, hearing those not so delightful encouraging words, Paul and I were able to reason together, that of course there would come little challenges, adjustments along the way, especially as you step out of your comfort zone for God. That's normal right?

We had no idea what those three little words would come to mean to us and our family as we journeyed through the six years we spent in Tasmania. "Tough times ahead."

Our camp continued throughout the weekend as expected. We didn't think much of those three little words again during this time. It was just great watching everyone really getting to know each other, leaning in to hear from God and being motivated for our church's road ahead. And I am happy to report, no more surprises for us! At least, not during that weekend.

After camp, everything continued as normal. Those three little words, "tough times ahead" was not raised again. Sure there were adjustments to be made, new ways of doing things, learning the lay of the land, helping our kids adjust to a new school, building new friendships and dare I say, learning to go back to half day Saturday, no Sunday shopping.

At that time in Hobart, shops closed on Saturday afternoon and all day Sunday. When I learnt this bit of news, my first thought was, what, what, what! No all weekend shopping! Seriously? Maybe this was my "tough times ahead?" Deb, you can do it.

Apart from these small adjustments, all in all, things were going well and according to plan. Within a couple of months we were finding our feet and looking forward to what the future would hold for us, life was good and we were starting to feel comfortable with our new surroundings.

5
TOUGH TIMES AHEAD

We were just three months in when those three little words began to surface. Those three little words, we had put on the shelf, "tough times ahead," began to filter into our lives in ways we did not expect. They began to shake our faith, shake our trust in decisions we had made and make us want to run!

Three months into this journey of ours, and only one month since the camp, we were to discover the business we had bought was not all it had been laid out to be on paper. Our clients had been cheated badly by the previous owner and the business name had been left with a bad reputation. We found ourselves having to dip into funds to prop up the business, funds we had set aside to buy a house. As Christians, we wanted to honour the promises made to our clients by the previous owner who had taken advantage of them financially. We thought if we poured honesty, goodwill and resource into our business, it would turn around. After all we came here in obedience to God so surely it would all work out.

We sent out letters to our clients to assure them that we would take care of them and give them the best service we could. We thought it was a very simple, good honest letter. Unfortunately, that letter got into the hands of the previous owner who took it as a slur against himself and he began to harass us over a twelve month period.

It began one day with a phone call. He rang our home number and started shouting down the phone at our twelve-year-old daughter Belinda, who had answered the call. "I am going to sue you for defamation of character." And from that day on, for over a year, he harassed us in many different ways including trying to destroy our credibility. Dealing with this, and other underlying issues with the business, we found ourselves having to pour more and more resource into it to stop the business going under.

As things began to fall apart with the business, other things started to come in on us as well. The pangs of homesickness for anything familiar came, particularly for family and old friends. The kids were also missing their friends and the reality of change hit us like a ton of bricks. We were not on holidays. We are living here. We couldn't just get in our car and drive back to our hometown Newcastle for a reprieve, because we were living on an island.

Over the next twelve months things continued to get harder financially and adjustments for us took longer than we thought, particularly for myself, and our daughter Belinda. Belinda began to grieve deeply for the life she had left behind in Newcastle. Being twelve years old, and transitioning from a young girl to a teenager, she found it very difficult to adjust to our new situation and it took a long time for her to come through. In Newcastle, she had many friends, but now she was finding it difficult to make even one new friend. Of course, this affected us also, watching her struggle through this time. How could we help her?

As funds started to dry up, we could no longer just go out, take our kids to anywhere, in fact! We had to start watching every dollar and found ourselves regularly having to say no to our children's requests, while all other kids were going places. This didn't make it any easier for them during their first twelve months of trying to fit in and make new friends. As a total socialite and life of any party, Josh found this particularly hard.

To understand where we had come from, in Newcastle we had a great business and Paul was an amazing provider. If we needed something or simply wanted anything extra for that matter, Paul would just go out and work more and we had it. Also with the previous business we were in, we were often going to fancy places with the company. There was an annual special dinner for high achievers called 'Join the Champions Dinner' and Paul always qualified for this. (Paul, you are my champion. Just had to throw that in.) This meant we would travel to Sydney, stay in a five star hotel, attend high-class functions and socialise with all the other achievers. Our functions were world class.

I remember one time the company hired all the ferries on Sydney Harbour for a ferry race, which was then followed by a dinner at Taronga Zoo. The company had booked the entire zoo for the evening. Yes, that's right, we had the whole zoo to ourselves. We were greeted by the staff and serenaded in by a famous band of the time. Awaiting us was the biggest barbeque we had ever seen and they deemed it as 'The biggest barbeque in the biggest backyard in Australia.' Then of course there were the clothes. None of this was complete without the expensive new outfits you just had to have. I shudder now remembering how much I paid for just one of those outfits. Not that I have a problem buying clothes, I have a black belt in buying clothes, but truly, this was overboard. At the time it seemed normal because the people we were around were the same. Our trip to Hawaii for one of our off shore conferences was no less impressive. Red carpet service all the way, from the time we got off the plane till the time we landed back home.

This life was becoming normal to us, so you can imagine the 'laid on' mindset we had. One time we went to a family camp with our church in Newcastle, and I didn't take towels. I emphasis, I, me, mwah, didn't pack them. I just assumed they would be supplied. Yes, I know what you are thinking. No more to be said about that! But you can see the distance between where we had come from to where we were now.

Sometimes we can be in danger of putting ourselves inside a bubble of a certain lifestyle that leaves no room for God. God can be around you, you can still love Him, serve Him and be committed to the service of Him and still not have Him in that first place that only He deserves. There is nothing wrong with being wealthy, having wonderful things, but we can't let a golden bubble become more important than our relationship with our eternal, beyond magnificent, creator God who truly does have our best interest at heart.

With our lifestyle now dramatically changed, we were finding ourselves not only not buying what we wanted, but instead, having to decide what we really needed the most. For example, when grocery shopping, we would use the small basket as opposed to the trolley. Doing a big shop was no longer an option for us. The thought of getting to the checkout counter and finding we didn't have enough money to pay for even the bare minimum was always a great fear for me. If I stuck to the basket, I was sure I would not over spend.

I did not want this way of shopping to become a stronghold of fear every time we went, so I started taking pen and paper to add up what we were buying along the way and this helped.

After the first three-month honeymoon period, we found ourselves, over the following twelve months, crying out to God daily as things continued to go from bad to worse. "Lord what is going on? We came here in Your will. We know You called us here. Please Lord, give us a breakthrough." My husband Paul would hold the Bible up to heaven and say to the Lord, "Your promises are true, what is happening here? We believe Your word, we stand on Your word."

Paul was an incredible provider and in Newcastle, was one of the best salesmen in his company. He knew what he had to do to get a sale as selling came naturally to him. Now, in a similar business, no matter what he did, how hard he tried, nothing was working. He would say to God, "I know what I have to do to get sales but nothing is happening. Why?"

After many months seeking God over this, Paul finally got his answer.

Not the one he was looking for, but then we were getting used to those kinds of answers. God said, "Paul, what you have been able to do in the past and what you are trying to do now, is not going to work anymore. I want you to come to a place where I become your total source of supply, for everything."

That sounded good, but the way we were feeling at this point, it was easier said than done. Any positive energy we had left, was poured into the church and our kids. There was nothing left for ourselves personally, to be able to stand strong with an optimistic perspective. As we were trying to build up other people, we found our own internal building blocks were crumbling.

From the time our "tough times ahead" season started and for the following twelve months, every day, seven days a week, we were living in this mode of stinking thinking, letting the enemy rule the very fibre of our being. We had arrived in Tasmania with such a victorious mindset, which had been so strong in us at the beginning, but little by little, without realising it, we were allowing everything that was coming upon us, to smother us. What a trap!

We finally came to the end of ourselves, to a place of having nowhere else to go but on our knees praying for a breakthrough to come. When we arrived at this place, there was God, who had been patiently waiting all this time, for us to meet Him there.

I remember this day so vividly. We got on our knees and cried out to God with all we had left in us, "Lord, we know that You called us here. We know You brought us to this place for Your purposes. We don't understand what is going on. Why all this is happening? What we do know is this: You are good, and You do good. You desire good for us and You love us completely, so whatever You are doing in us, just do it. We don't want to go around the mountain another day." Finally we got it but it took us twelve months to come to this revelation.

After praying that prayer did God give us a full description of His plan beginning to end in this rollercoaster season? No! Did our situation change? No, not initially. Something more significant happened, we changed!

God answered our prayers, not by breaking the back of our circumstances, but by breaking us. Not to destroy us, but to build us up in our faith in Him, and help us develop resilience for the seasons ahead. Little did we know at this time, He had an even greater purpose in mind that He wanted to entrust to us but there was much work to be done in us before this could take place.

A dangerous prayer to pray! Whatever you are doing in us, just do it! But this has to be the place we all come to. To be willing to say YES to God, no matter what!

I know what you are thinking right now. "So, if I want to follow the calling and passion of God, I am going to have to be broken. If I start walking this path of God's will, get out of my comfortable chair like you are asking me to, place myself at the centre of God's calling, I have to be broken, I have to go through stuff?"

I have to answer, "YES," and some of us need more breaking than others. Especially us strong-minded, independent, 'I know how to do things' kind of people. Yep, there will be some breaking, but it will be worth it. I can stand here today and say, from personal experience, that absolutely, it is worth it.

It will be beneficial to you and for you, and fruit will burst forth from inside of you that you didn't even know was there. God fruit. John 15:2 tells us very clearly there will be some breaking (pruning) - He cuts off every branch in me that bears no fruit, while every branch that does bear fruit he prunes, so that it will bear even more fruitful. The much-needed scripture we love to hate. This scripture is two fold. Basically we will be pruned if we do and pruned if we don't, so let's allow God to prune us in our obedience rather than in our disobedience.

After a year of wallowing in our self-pity, God had our attention in the right way. For the previous twelve months, we had been too busy feeling sorry for ourselves. Our language was 'poor us.' Poor us, look at the situation we are in. Poor us, we do the right thing and this is what we get. Poor us, we don't have our comfortable friends, or our extended family with us. Poor us, we don't have enough money. Poor us, we don't have a house to call our own any more and maybe not ever again. Poor us, we don't understand our new 'culture' nor do they understand us. Oh, poor us.

Unless we let God break us, we will stay in that 'poor me, poor us' state forever, never moving forward. Either God is God or He is not. And I can say with confidence, God truly is, who He says He is. He is our strong tower, our deliverer, He is our provider, He is our Father and God of the possible and the impossible. We have to trust God no matter what, even when circumstances seem unstable. My husband Paul often shares the following example of trust.

A man by the name of Charles Blondin, became famous in 1859 when he attempted to be the first person to cross the Niagara Falls on a tightrope. The tightrope was stretched over approximately 400 metres (quarter of a mile) from one side to the other and was 48 metres (160 feet) above the falls. He attempted this feat on several occasions and on each crossing, he would do something more challenging. One time he crossed in a sack, another time on stilts, then on a bicycle, even in the dark, and once he even carried a stove and cooked an omelet in the middle of the tightrope! As crowds gathered, they cheered him on and often their roar was louder than the powerful flowing water cascading over the falls. By now, word was out and the crowds were growing. They waited with great anticipation at what Charles would do next and Charles never did disappoint. On this occasion, he blindfolded himself, took a wheelbarrow and crossed the tightrope effortlessly. The roar was deafening and the crowd now totally believed in his ability. As he reached the other side, he called out to all those fans who were watching from the river bank, "Do you believe I can carry a person across in this wheelbarrow?" The crowd enthusiastically shouted, "Yes, yes, yes. You are the greatest tightrope walker in the world. You can do anything!" "Okay," said Blondin, "I ask for a volunteer to get into the wheelbarrow and I will wheel you across." And you guessed it, no one put their hand up!

We can believe God's word to be true, we can cheer from the river bank and declare our trust in God, saying, "Yes I am going to put my life in Your hands, to take me where You want to lead me. I will not hold back." However, when it comes to God asking us to get into that wheelbarrow, are we willing to do it?

We have to be willing to not only get into the wheelbarrow, but stay in it for the whole journey, even when we feel we are way out of our depth. As talented and capable as Charles Blondin was, he does not compare to our talented, capable God who is more, way more able to do the impossible and keep us from falling. Your job, get into the wheelbarrow and stay there. God's job is to steer it. Seriously, can you imagine trying to wheel the barrow while at the same time sitting in it? It's not going to work for you.

Thank God, we came to a point as a family where we bowed before God and said, "We're in. Even when our nails may at times clutch the sides of that barrow, we promise we will not jump out. Just do what you need to do in us."

From that point on, there was a complete turn around - in us. Now we were getting serious about submission to God. Before, we were submissive as long as we could add up the numbers, because in our mind, they needed to add up for us to move forward. Now, it didn't matter, not because we didn't care, but our cares were in the right hands. When we learnt to submit our whole life, our will and emotions to God, we became acquainted with Him at a whole new level. He became our closest friend and confidant, our strength and comforter, our total source of finance and our solid rock. Was it always easy? No. Did we always like it? Of course not! Did we falter at times? You bet. We are still human in need

> God, we know you have called us to this place, we don't know what You are doing, but whatever You want to do in us, ***just do it.***

of a Savior every single day, but every day we chose to get back up and keep moving forward.

After our baptism of revelation, clarity came to us about that 'knock me down' prophesy we received on our arrival. These three directives and revelations were very clear:

1. I have called you. *Stay focused on what I have called you here for.*
2. Don't look to the right or left. *There will be distractions, things you won't understand. Don't let them entangle you. Don't let them consume you. (Guilty)!*
3. There are tough times ahead. *I am telling you right at the outset so don't be surprised when they come. If I am telling you about it, then you have to know I know it from beginning to end which means, I am in this with you and I have solutions to every situation.*

If we want to be used effectively long term, we have to be willing to let God sandpaper us how He chooses. Sandpaper is for one purpose and one purpose only, to smooth the rough edges off something to create a beautiful finished product. When we have the choice between two identical items in a shop one sandpapered and polished and one that is not, of course we are going to buy the one that looks finished. Let's allow God get the job done in us because when we are polished, and only then, can people see a reflection, the God reflection in us!

I think I have made my point, but if you would like it a little clearer, let me put it this way: stop whinging and let God do what He needs to do in you. It is for the best, your best. The sooner you submit, the sooner the job will be done!

Remember He wants to only do you good.

6
BREAKING OUT OF THE SHELL

Anyone who knows me, knows I can talk. I love to talk and I love to preach, but it wasn't always that way. When we lived in Newcastle, my husband was the manager of a team at the company he worked for and sometimes we had to go to high society events as I mentioned before. No one would know it, but I feared going to these events and often would say to Paul, "Please don't leave me alone, I don't want to talk to anyone." Although I had dealt with my past to a degree, I was still growing in self worth; however, thoughts of past ridicule would sometimes haunt me.

If we are not careful, thoughts like those can get in the way of hearing God's truth about what He has deposited in us. I remember one such incident that caused me to listen to my own thoughts instead of God's. We had just finished a team meeting that Paul was running, and I noticed one of the team members had not been listening so I reiterated to him what Paul had shared and immediately he came right up to my face and said, "Who do you think you are? Do you think you are the boss? Don't tell me what to do!" Those words went straight into my heart and it created the label 'I'm bossy' in me that I wore for a long time. Not wanting to be thought of as bossy, I withdrew.

Thank goodness God knew my potential and true title. He needed to sandpaper that old label right out of me, so sandpapering He did, and this is how it unfolded.

As the business we bought in Tasmania could no longer support us, but rather continued to take us further into decline and deeper into debt, I had to make the decision to get a job. Although I had worked alongside Paul in his business in Newcastle, I didn't have the responsibility of being the breadwinner. I could come and go as I pleased. I didn't have to worry about finances because, as I said before, Paul was doing an amazing job of providing for us all. I was happy with my life, being a wife and mother at home, on the music team at our church (I could hide behind a keyboard), teaching dance at the school (kids were ok) and enjoying our close circle of friends on the weekends whom we had been with through thick and thin for many years. I was in my comfort zone. Everything was as I liked it.

Having to make the decision to find independent work to help support the family was a scary thought but I knew I had no choice. It wasn't that I was not willing to work or work hard because Paul and I are wired that way. It was more the thought of what could I do or, more to the point, what could I do comfortably?

Paul was doing his very best through the business, but of course that was not working for us. I knew I had to do something, but what? Although, before having our children, I had worked in a bank, I knew working in an institution like that again would not give me the freedom I needed to be around for Belinda and Josh when they came home from school, which was very important to me. I prayed and asked God, "Please Lord, help me find a job that will be suitable for me." When you pray a prayer like that, you have to be open to what God gives you. In my mind, when I asked God to give me a suitable job, I meant something that I liked and that was within my comfort zone. God did give me a suitable job, but His suitable and my suitable were two different things. I wanted something where I could sit in the background, quietly doing a job and go home. God's idea was completely different.

Not too long after that prayer, I found out about a job demonstrating new products in supermarkets. I didn't actually know what the job entailed but at the interview I was told I would need to talk to people, engage them and sell the product to them. All I heard was *talk*. Talk to people, talk to strangers, talk to the public. "Are you kidding God? You know I don't like to speak in public places."

My mind went into a backspin and memories of the past came flooding in like a movie being played out afresh before my eyes. People will laugh at me. People will say, "Don't you tell me what to do (to buy)!"

But God gently reminded me of the pact Paul and I had made with Him when we were on our knees, "Whatever you are doing in us, just do it." So despite how I was feeling, I let my roller coaster emotions give way to trust. Trust that if God was providing the work, He would also give me the confidence and ability I needed to do the job.

I am so glad I listened to the voice of God that day, rather than the voice of doubt that was trying so hard to interfere with my decision. God spoke very clearly to my spirit, "Deb, this is the door I am opening for you, walk through it."

You can imagine my first day! I was a bundle of nerves, I had no idea how I was going to open my mouth to beckon people to come and try my product line but I was determined not to do "a Moses" who said to God, "Get someone else, I can't speak." I told myself, "I can do this!" Fortunately, God was gracious enough to put my demonstration stand right next to my friend for the first shift. She helped me learn the ropes of meeting with the boss of the store, setting up and preparing the product. However, the demonstrating and selling of the product was totally up to me. My friend couldn't be running between two stations and God, although He was with me, was not going to do it on my behalf. He knew the gifting He'd placed inside of me, and now He was placing me in a situation where it had to come out.

I needed to step out of my comfort zone and 'do it afraid.' I had to talk. The company I worked for marketed all types of products, ranging from food to new home labour-saving devices. I was thankful that my first shift was demonstrating food. Although I was nervous and not a lover of cooking, I had two things on my side: I actually could cook and I knew humans loved to eat. This made my first experience much easier. So that first day, I cooked, smiled and with a trembling voice, offered tasty treats to everyone who passed by. To my surprise, everyone accepted and a few even asked where they could purchase the product. At the end of that first day, my confidence had grown and I left with a sense of great satisfaction. Not only had I made it through the day, but I actually spoke to strangers and on top of that, I was contributing to our family's financial needs.

Over the next few weeks, I became more and more confident in the job and believe it or not, started to enjoy speaking to people. Not only this, but as time went on, I found myself becoming quite competitive. I was no longer satisfied just meeting quota, but found myself with a growing passion to sell more than anyone else in the store. Each week I would try to beat my previous record of sales with the goal of being top salesperson of the week. I knew I had a competitive spirit (which can be both good and bad, depending on attitude), but as I began to top the sales most weeks, I could see that God was strengthening my core and building something into me.

Sometimes we can question what God puts on our plate. "Are you sure about this God? Is this really what you want me to do?" But I have learnt, and continue to learn that God is trustworthy and He knows what He is doing.

Well, I stayed in that job for sixteen months, and over that time, I grew a lot. I even got promoted to become the boss's assistant. Who would have thought, just a short sixteen months previously, when I sheepishly tiptoed into that first supermarket that I would have been in the position I found myself very soon after.

God uses every life experience to do something good in us, bring something out of us or thrust us into something that we didn't know we could do and this is what God was doing for me when He led me into this field. Yes, it was a job to make some money for our family but I believe that even beyond this, His purpose was to develop in me the confidence to speak. He had put a speaking gift inside of me that needed to be pulled out and to do that He needed to grow my confidence in speaking.

Demonstrating in supermarkets and other shops was His 'school of learning' for me. I had no idea that this was what God was doing at the time nor did I know what He had in store for me in the years to come. This school of life was readying me for not only our mission calling, but also for public speaking. I can say today, with all my heart, I am so grateful that I listened and obeyed, so this gifting could be brought out in me.

I had just packed up from another day at work and was about to walk out the door, when I suddenly sensed the presence of God on and around me. I stopped in my tracks, turned around, and there, in the middle of the supermarket, God spoke very clearly to me. He said, "Deb, your demonstrating days are over." For the first time in sixteen months after working in countless shopping centres, I felt a shift take place in my spirit and I knew I didn't belong here anymore. Continuing my conversation with God in this most unorthodox place, I said, "God, if I am finished here, now what?" And true to God's form, all He said was, "It is time to move on."

It's time to move on?

"What does that mean God?" And He answered me with this, "Deb, you have successfully completed your apprenticeship. You stepped out of your comfort zone, and now you are in a place where you are willing to speak to anyone about anything, anywhere. From now on you will speak for Me. You will use your voice for My purposes, but there is still more sandpapering to be done in you before then." Great! And oh great!

Great, because I had broken through the bondage of fear of speaking, which for so long had controlled me, and, 'oh great,' because there were still more furnace experiences to come. Just like the polished teapot on the shelf, I knew the end result would be worth it so again I said YES to God.

To keep moving forward we have to be willing to let God complete in us what He started. We can go through one learning experience and say, "Hey God, that's enough, I've grown and I'm good right here thanks very much." But if we really want to be all that God has created us to be, we need to let Him complete the work. Trust Him in the journey and stay in that wheelbarrow!

Although my demonstrating in supermarket days were behind me, my working days were not. Our financial situation still had not changed so I knew I had to find other employment.

I did not know what God had in mind for me next but I was sure of two things; it would put me in a position of further personal growth for more sandpapering to be done, and it would be a source of provision for my family.

The wages I received while demonstrating were, in the natural, never quite enough to put food on our table, pay school fees for our kids, rent for our house, petrol for our car, phone and electricity bills or any of those other things we associate with everyday living and yet week after week we made it. Not once did we go hungry, not once did our electricity get cut off or did we run out of petrol. That was not to say we weren't extremely careful with every dollar, doing our best to be wise with what we had, but no matter how careful we were, seriously, in the natural, what came in did not add up to the amount that went out. How could this be? I'm glad you asked.

Let' talk for a minute about that 'in the natural' statement I just made. Throughout this six year refining season, God did not just sandpaper us, He also proved Himself over the top, out of the box, beyond imagination, our provider, supplier of every need and opened doors in many 'unnatural' ways.

If there is anything I have learnt in this journey of life thus far, it is that

God can be relied upon in whatever circumstances that come our way. As humans, in our own fleshly mind, we try and figure out what needs to be done for things to work out right. We then stress over it when it doesn't look like it is going to plan, only to find ourselves grabbing at straws in order to come up with a solution, and more often than not, end up with second best.

Our finite mind can only think up certain ways of how to get to our intended goal, but thankfully, we serve an infinite God whose ways are higher than our ways and whose thoughts are higher than our thoughts. So I think He might have a clue about how to work it all out! What do you think?

Of course, we must do whatever we can do in the natural because God doesn't want us to just sit back either and think, "Oh God, it is all up to You." It is very clear in James 2:22, which tells us our works and faith, must operate together, or our faith is dead in the water. I always say, work like it all depends on you, doing what you can in the natural and at the same time, be listening for God's lead, and trusting He has got this.

The part we play can be, for example, through working overtime or selling something, if the need is financial, or if it is deciding between taking this job or that job. Put your options on the table and start moving forward on the decision that looks right and see how God will start to move in your situation, directing your path.

Proverbs 16:9 tells us very clearly, you make your plans and God will direct your steps. We can't just wait for a bolt of lightning to strike from heaven and land on a map as if to say, "Go ye this way." I am not saying that this can't happen, but I wouldn't hold my breath for that one. You must make your plans. In other words God is saying, I gave you a brain to think, so use it and I will come in on the mix and start directing those plans. So work like it depends on you, but trust, have faith and acknowledge God like it all depends on Him. That's how our God works.

For us, our 'out of the box' God, provided beyond my part time, basic salary, in many different ways. There were times it came in the form of leftover demonstrating products given to us. Often it was food and occasionally household products but always what we needed at the time. Sometimes it came by way of car-pooling our kids to get to school. And bread! We never ran out of bread as our church received mountains of it weekly from a local shop. Then there were the dinner invitations that would come at times we weren't sure what we would feed our kids and even though our business was failing, being a hair salon related business, we could always get free haircuts.

There were so many different ways that God provided. Ways we couldn't have orchestrated even if we tried. For example, a letter arrived in the mail one day for a free car service, a car service for Subaru cars and yes, you guessed it, our car was a Subaru and it definitely needed a service. There were big things and little things, too numerous to mention them all, but things that made the difference between us making it, or not.

I remember when God even multiplied food supernaturally. We often had people over for Sunday lunch because we wanted to get to know everyone in our church on a more personal basis. Every Sunday people knew what was on the menu, pumpkin soup and our free bread. I believe my pumpkin soup was the best because I had the most practice at it. Fortunately everyone loved pumpkin soup. It was perfect for the Tasmanian climate and I was confident that I could provide enough for any amount of people because pumpkin, potato and onion were cheap. Even when extra people arrived on our doorstep those Sundays, the pot of soup never ran out until all were full.

One Sunday evening, we decided to invite our church leadership over for dinner without processing the fact that we actually didn't have anything left in the house to feed them. The proposal for dinner had popped out of my mouth before I knew it and they had accepted. We had already done the pumpkin soup lunch thing, which meant no more pumpkins. The minute church finished, we left so we could rush home to find something that wasn't there. Our drive home had us praying fervently "Help God, what can we give them?" I couldn't get in the door quick enough as I had to produce something, before our guests arrived to sit at our 'banquet' table. I opened the cupboards and shut them just as quickly. I already knew there was nothing in there, but I did it anyway just hoping something would appear. I opened the fridge and again, nothing. I then opened the freezer and yes, there it was, our so-called five loaves and two fish. In the corner of our freezer lay a lone sausage. Just one. I was so excited to find it, but at the same time I was thinking what could I do with one sausage? I didn't have time to deliberate about what fancy dish I could come up with, so I quickly thawed it out and fried it. I also found a handful of rice, and of course you know we had bread. That wonderful, free bread! I cooked up that sausage and sliced it as thin as possible to make it look like much more and managed to produce a meal for our guests. As I served them with a smile, my heart was still racing, but at the same time, I was thanking God for making something out of nothing. That night, we not only ate, but everyone was full. This was not possible in the natural but, with God…! It is quite comical now playing it back in my mind as I write this, but not so amusing at the time. It is, however, a perfect example of God doing beyond what we can ask or imagine. Trust Him and keep saying YES.

BACK TO THE BANK

God, where to from here? A question I had been asking since God told me my demonstrating days were over and today, He answered me. I again instinctively heard God speak as clearly as He did when telling me to leave demonstrating, "Apply for a job in the bank."

I had not done banking since having our first child, thirteen years previously. It was not something I ever expected to be going back to. I only knew one person in Tasmania who worked in the bank as my previous experience was only in Newcastle. Thankfully that one person I knew went to our church. When Sunday came around I asked her if there were any jobs available in her bank. She said, "My bank has been advertising for bank tellers for the past few months, but the cut-off date to get applications in has just closed and we already have ninety applicants to fill just four positions." But then she said, "I will get you a form anyway, fill it in and we will pray."

The odds were stacked against me. I hadn't worked in a bank for over thirteen years, I didn't know anything about being a bank teller as my previous job was in administration and I was far too late submitting my application. Besides all this, there were already ninety other applicants bidding for only four positions.

However, in my spirit, I just knew I was going to get one of those four positions. It was not a natural belief, but a supernatural knowing to the point that anything could have been against me that day and in the

> The one who calls you is faithful, He will do it.
> 1 Thessalonians 5:24 (NLT)
>
> In other words, if God is in it, He is in it. God will make it happen

days ahead while waiting to get word for an interview, and it would not have shaken my faith. And as you have probably already guessed, I did get an interview and I did get one of those four positions. And, not only that, it was at the branch closest to where we lived. It was a miracle. God is so amazing. It was the perfect part-time job because not only was it ten minutes drive from our house, but this job gave me flexibility to be home for our kids after school, and at the same time there was plenty of opportunity to take overtime shifts if I wanted them. This job served me well over what was going to be the next four-plus years.

7
WHAT IS MISSIONS ANYWAY?

Missions is something that grabbed Paul's and my heart early in our married life. We assumed our future would be on the mission field or at least in mission-related work. Our home church in Newcastle had a very strong focus on Sri Lanka so we assumed that this would be where we'd end up. However, through the series of events you now know, here we were, in Tasmania, on Australian soil rather than overseas soil, and although we didn't fully understand why, we accepted that this was the mission field God wanted us to be planted in.

The word mission means calling, purpose, duty, responsibility and the word missionary means disciple, follower, one sent on a mission. So the bottom line is, we are all called to be messengers with a responsibility to our calling, whatever or wherever that is, to reach people and connect people to God.

In Tasmania, we were often asked, "So how long are you going to stay here?" And we would always answer, "As long as God wants us to; it could be forever." This was a common question locals asked people coming from the mainland, because although many would come, few would stay. We really had no idea how long God wanted us to stay in Tasmania but we had to plant ourselves as though we were here forever. If we didn't do that, we couldn't truly give one hundred percent to what God was calling us here for. Nor would our hearts be truly open to the people around us or to the work God was doing in us. If we didn't give it our all, we would always be looking for the next whatever, and that would not be fair to all involved. To God, others and even ourselves.

Plan for the future, absolutely. Don't stay stagnant. God wants us to keep developing, growing and building, but it is vital that we dig in where we are planted. This was the decision we took when God not only called us to Tasmania to partner with Him in the work of the church but also in allowing Him to work in us personally throughout the difficult times and in particular, the area of financial despair.

We have to see every season, every experience, every lesson as building blocks for our lives. Don't let any of it spill to the ground, for all of it is valuable, and none of it is wasted in the hands of God.

Our knees became well acquainted with the floor through those times and our faith grew as well as our hunger for God to keep working on us. You have to be careful when you pray prayers like, "Whatever you are doing in us, just do it," because He will give you what you ask for. So again and again, He'd put us back on the rack to do more stretching, more sandpapering, more leaning in to Him, and the more stretching that took place, the more we found ourselves on our knees praying those deep prayers. You know the ones I mean

> In times of needing to dig in deep with God, you get to really know Him. The results are incomparable. Trust, peace, faith and real connection. You can't get them anywhere else.

right? "God, help!" but it was in those times, those cry out intimate times with God, seeking His face for wisdom, for grace, for mercy, for comfort, for provision, for insight, for every thing we needed, that we got to know God. I mean, really got to know God. There is nothing better or more satisfying than getting closer to God. The results are incomparable. Trust, peace, faith and real connection. You can't get this anywhere else.

All the while God worked on us, building a stronger core and character, we were also seeing the church grow from strength to strength. It was exciting to watch this tiny church grow from small beginnings to one that was healthy, vibrant and expanding. Being a new work, filled with lots of young people and young families, it kept the church motivated to evolve and reach out to the community. It was worth every moment of being in a place that was not originally our hometown and as we grew to love this place and to love the people, we also found ourselves adopting it as our home. Still to this day, we have a strong love and connection to this beautiful island state called Tasmania.

A SPRING IN THE DESERT

By 1994, we had lost absolutely everything. All our savings, money from the sale of our Newcastle home, our insurance, everything. We had poured it all into our failing business in hopes of turning it around. We were not ones to give up so easily! As a woman, a wife and mum, one nagging thought was gnawing at me. "Would we ever have our own home again?"

As women, we love to create a home environment wherever we are, and this applies to both married and single gals. Guys are happy with just a bed and a fridge, but for us gals, we want a bit more comfort than that. We have to at least have hot running water and fluffy pillows. It is just something in us and if we are married, we want the lot. We want to make it a comfortable nest for our family, transforming it from a house to a home. Make it a fun filled environment for kids, and a safe haven to return to. Even if we are not wired to be full time stay at home mums, there is something in us that desires to create a home base.

I can say with conviction that I was always, always there for our kids during their growing up years in every way, but I am not your typical stay at home, homemaker. I knew God had put the call of ministry in me, so although I did do the domestic thing and I liked everything in its place, I was not 'Miss Domestic' by nature. When God did eventually call us to overseas missions, to Vietnam, and I found out that you were expected to have a house help to clean and cook, I definitely knew I was called. Haha! If ever there was a doubt in my mind about the call, that vital bit of information settled it. If you talk to my husband, he will tell you, "I didn't marry her for her cooking skills." I would like to add though, I can cook…if I must.

Well I said all that to say this, whether you are called to be a stay at home mum, a ministry working or business working mum, there is a part of us all that wants to create a safe haven we call home for ourselves, and for our families. During this season for me, our ministry was growing and even glimpses of future overseas ministry were coming into view, but as a mum and a wife, watching all our assets disappear, often took my thoughts to that place of the possibility of never having our own house again.

Although we had begun to call Tasmania home, still, we were living in a state that was not our home state, living in a home that was not our own and at times I felt like we were living transiently. Yes we had definitely planted ourselves firmly here and yes we were one hundred percent committed but a little part of me kept saying to God, "If we could just have a home of our own here, I could truly make a nest for our family."

At the time, it was a huge deal for me and God knew this so He took a sympathetic view of this with me. He reminded me of the fact, He knew how I felt and of course He did! If anyone could understand, it was God through His son Jesus Christ. Jesus, who was thrust into our world from His, His homeland heaven, to be born in a dwelling that was not His own, nor comfortable for that matter and to live and minister among strangers. Yes, I knew He understood and that I had His ear.

One Sunday evening in that same year of my conversation with

God about my need for a home of our own, the Australian Christian Churches (ACC) NSW State President at the time, previously known as Assemblies of God (AOG) was in town speaking at Hobart AOG. Our church, along with other churches, joined with Hobart AOG to hear this pastor speak. At the end of his message, he asked people to come out for prayer. Prayer for salvation, for healing and for any other needs. We were so excited to see many go to the front of the church for prayer, especially those who had just made a commitment to accept Jesus into their lives. As this pastor began to pray, we extended our hands forward to agree together with his prayers for God to come and do His work in these precious people.

Our speaker had just finished praying for one or two of the many who were out in front, and as he moved towards the next person in line, he suddenly stopped. This made me look up and at the very same moment, I sensed the Holy Spirit come upon me. In that same instant, the speaker pointed to me and said these words, "God is going to give you the desires of your heart and it is going to be in a miraculous way." He then turned, and without missing a beat, continued praying for all the others who had stood seeking a touch from God.

It was just a moment in time, no special prayer nor explanation but I knew in my heart without a shadow of a doubt, that this was a house. That one day, God was going to give us our own house and it would be in a miraculous way.

Ephesians 3:20 (NIV) says, "Now to Him who is able to do immeasurably more than all we ask or imagine, according to His power that is at work within us, to Him be glory in the church and in Christ Jesus throughout all generations, for ever and ever! Amen."

He gives us more than we can ask or imagine. My mind had planned it all out in the only way my finite mind could. Get another mortgage and somehow pay a house off, but God is so much greater that this. His ways are higher than my ways, His thoughts are higher than my thoughts and also His timing is always perfect. He says it will be a home given miraculously. I can let my mind wander on how this could be but

I am not going to do that. He said it, so He will do it, and He will do it His way. It was now settled in my spirit and it no longer needed to occupy my mind.

We didn't get to own a house in Tasmania, but looking back now, I see so clearly that this would not have been a good thing for us. God did not want us to be so nestled in, so comfortable, that we would find ourselves unwilling to let go when He wanted us to move on. At the time, we had no idea that our Tasmanian season would only be for six years. We didn't realise that God was planting in us greater things for a greater destiny, therefore settling into a lovely comfortable lifestyle in Tasmania, as beautiful as it was, would not have satisfied us anyway.
So as I write this, you are probably wondering, if we have that house yet? No we don't but that is OK because we don't need it yet and I am not worried about it either. I know that when the time is right, we will have a house of our own and God will provide it.

FUTURE REVEALED

Again, in that same year of 1994, on the 14th of October, we found ourselves on a collision course with our future destiny. On this day, our church combined with many others to began a week-long missions summit. The only information we had about the guest speaker was that he was an American and he was doing ministry in Asia. Our motivation for going to these meetings was for our church to gain a stronger passion for missions.

We had no idea what was about to happen to us during that very first meeting. It was totally unexpected because our focus was on seeing our church being inspired by a real life missionary and in turn to see missions as a way of life, both on home soil and abroad. We should have known better! That something would stir in our own hearts, after all missions was in our DNA!

After introducing himself, telling us a little of his background and how he came to be involved in overseas ministry, this missionary began to share about the plight of the youth and children in Vietnam. As he spoke of their daily life, the struggles and the sense of hopelessness they faced, it hit both Paul and my hearts like a ton of bricks. God spoke to us both at the same time saying, "This is what I am calling you to." It was so strong, so undeniable, that we turned to each other at the same time, and without saying a word, we just knew, this was our destiny. It was like someone had come along and injected us with a powerful drug that awakened sensations in us, a passion that refused to shift and from that moment on, our hearts and minds were totally changed for the ordinary. The sense of God's call on our lives became unshakable.

After those meetings, our church decided that some of us must go and see for ourselves what was happening in this nation. A nation that was so unknown to us and yet to the world, was known as a country of war. A war that we found ourselves watching from afar through our television screens. Everyone knew about it. It was the very first war to ever come into our living rooms as it was happening. We weren't just reading about it in the newspaper, or listening to it on the radio, there were images, real life images that showed the raw reality of war. We were not watching some television drama series made up of actors that could take a break when the director said cut. These were images of lives living real war and we too, were now being impacted by the reality of battle on another level, the pain and suffering that so many men, women and children were enduring.

What could we do? Now the war was well and truly over, what part could we play in making a difference in this nation? We could not solve every problem but we could not stand by and do nothing either. Whatever was in our power to do, to make life better for the many ones, tens, hundreds or thousands, in some way we had to be willing to say, YES.

8
THAT FIRST TRIP

The planning began for our very first missions trip from the church and of course, the destination was Vietnam! Paul and I agreed together that it would be best if he went on this maiden trip while I stayed home with our children. At the time, it was just the most practical decision to make as a family and I was more than happy for him to go, for him to be the one to scout out the land for what could possibly be our next season, to taste and see if this really was the place for us, the country we still knew so little about yet found our hearts being drawn toward.

Knowing one of us must go was unquestionable, but how God was going to provide for the trip was altogether a different story. We knew we had to put the James 2:22 principle into action, so we began to use what was in our hands and the first thing we did was to sell things. Doing all we could in the natural and believing God to do what we couldn't.

James 2:22 (NIV) says, "You see that his faith and his actions were working together, and his faith was made complete by what he did."

It is worth being reminded of this scripture over and over again because if we truly put our faith in what God is saying here, we can confidently say YES to His leading, knowing He will work with us and it will be made complete.

Paul is not a sports fanatic, but he loves his scuba diving and in the past, he would go diving at every opportunity. In our lucrative days, he even scuba dived in the oceans of Hawaii and Fiji. You could tell by the look on his face after each adventure, he was in seventh heaven. The sights he experienced while deep within the ocean were spectacular. Swimming alongside the multitudes of colourful and varied fish, both large and small, observing amazing creatures that hid behind rocks, and enjoying the natural beauty that lay on the ocean bed never ceased to amaze him no matter how many times he went out. Tasmania was no different. It too, was one of the most stunning places on earth to dive, so whenever Paul could manage it, he would go with friends out to the deep waters to again swim amongst the magnificence of the aquatic world.

As we began doing an inventory of what we had in our house to sell, the first thing that came up was Paul's precious scuba gear. This alone could pay for the ticket. I knew if Paul was to sell this, it would be like selling a piece of himself. However, as big as Paul's passion was for scuba diving, his desire to go on this trip was even greater so without hesitation, he put an ad in the paper and it sold straight away.

> Jesus said, "Mark my words, no one who sacrifices house, brothers, sisters, mother, father, children, land because of me and the Message will lose out. They'll get it all back, but multiplied many times in homes, brothers, sisters, mothers, children, and land—but also in troubles. And then the bonus of eternal life!"
>
> Mark 10:29-31(MSG)

We cannot lose when we put God's business first!

God knows when we give or give sacrificially, with a right heart, right motive. He remembers it all and He cannot go against His word. We serve a generous God, beyond measure. When we hold on tightly to the things we know we are to surrender, we miss out on the blessings that surrender brings. Not only what we will receive in the natural but also in the spiritual.

There is something freeing when we surrender to God, whether that be material things, time, finance, your giftings or anything else. These things put into the hands of God will be more effective than in your own hands.

After giving up his prize possession, Paul began receiving money from all over the place. It was incredible, and when it was time to fly out for that month long trip to Vietnam, he had everything he needed.

On the 2nd February, 1995, at 1:10pm, Paul and seven others from our church flew out to what would be for us personally, the start of a destiny we were yet to realise. There were so many questions in Paul's mind as he left that day. What would he experience? How would he be greeted in this land that had only just opened up to the west? Would it be welcoming? Would it be as we had seen on the television screen? In a matter of hours, Paul would touch the soil of a nation that was to grab our hearts and our lives for many years to come.

As I write this now, I am reading Paul's journal entry about his first day walking the streets of Hanoi. He writes of his confrontation with poverty, the noise, multitudes of people living life on the streets, beggars asking for food or money. A life so far removed from what we in the west considered normal. It reminded me of the fact that ninety percent of the world do not live like Australians live. As Australians, no matter what things we may disagree with in our nation, we truly are a blessed one.

The noise, the traffic, the congestion, life on the streets, people and bicycles were everywhere he looked. Yes, bicycles. If you have visited Vietnam in recent years, or seen the many tourist brochures advertising Vietnam as a great holiday destination, you will know that the main mode of transport for many people is a bicycle or a motorbike. Today, as the country develops we are seeing more cars than ever before. The streets have improved, life has improved for many and there has been rapid growth over the past nineteen years but in 1995 it was a very different story. If you could afford it, your family owned just one bicycle, the lucky ones had two. If not, you took public transport or a cyclo taxi. A cyclo (Xich Lô) is a three-wheeled bicycle taxi. You sit at the front while the driver peddles behind you.

These days, flying around the world is much more accessible and our knowledge and adaptability to different cultures is much easier. This is due to Internet access, cheap airfares and of course, multiculturalism. But in those days, we had less understanding of each country. Little was known about the lifestyle of other nations except for the limited information we got through travel agencies, newspapers or television.

Paul loved every new experience and soaked in every moment. His first visit to the local market fascinated him as he walked past all the fresh meat lined up ready to be sold. Did I say fresh! Yes, it was as fresh as it could come! This meat was still alive! Want to buy a chicken? No problem, just give the trader a moment and she will have that fowl's head off and plucked in no time. It was same for the ducks that were kept in cane cages ready for sale. Other meats, such as buffalo and pork, they were hung up like Christmas decorations on hooks after being killed earlier that day. There was no part of the animal wasted, right down to their… you know whats! Everything was sold, cooked and eaten.

After the first few days getting acquainted with the city, the team then moved on to a remote village several hours away which was to be the main focus of their trip. Here they worked in a Centre for the Handicapped and also a Centre for Displaced Children. During Paul's time working with the locals and interacting with these amazing kids, his heart was being broken and an insatiable love came upon him for the Vietnamese people.

As I read the last page of Paul's journal, his final entry before returning home on the 1st March 1995, his closing words said this, "Mission Vietnam Complete, but I think it is only the beginning."
Little did he know just how much those words "only the beginning," were going to become a reality just two short years down the track.

When Paul arrived home, he was different. It was like only half of him came back to us. It wasn't that he didn't fully engage with us his family, but his heart was now bleeding for a people he had left behind. The Vietnamese people! The entire time Paul was in Vietnam he didn't experience any cultural stress at all, in fact he immersed himself in it, loving it all, but when he returned to us, his stress came in the form of what is known as reverse culture stress (or culture shock) and this was from seeing with fresh eyes our western opulence.

A day or so after his return, we went grocery shopping. I hadn't noticed it at first, but as we walked up and down each aisle, one by one, Paul was scanning the supermarket shelves, looking intently at how full each one was, noticing that it not only sold every product you can imagine, but multiple brands of each one. It was there it hit him. He stopped in the middle of one of the aisles and said, "Deb, it's too much, it's too much. We have so much, and Vietnam has nothing, I need to get out of here." We finished up our shopping as soon as we could so we could leave the store.

Most people, when experiencing a new culture, particularly an undeveloped one for the first time, will go through some form of culture stress and it is very real. For each individual it will be different, and we cannot dismiss his or her struggle as trivial. A single situation may cause anxiety for one but for someone else, it is interesting or even funny. We must take it seriously and help them process what they have just experienced because it may be your turn next.

I personally describe culture stress as experiences that we are trying to process but there is no place for them to land in our mind. They are like files trying to fit into a filing cabinet but there is no such place for that new sight, smell or situation so we become tense. In our own environment, we see or experience something that is familiar, that's normal to us and it slips into the right spot with ease. But when we experience something that is not in our system, we don't have a file for it, it has nowhere to go so we experience stress until we have processed it. Once we have done that, our mind makes room for a new file and it slides in nicely. This may happen quickly or over time, but it will happen.

9
LEAVING THINGS IN OUR HANDS

We had been working together with the senior pastors of our Hobart church for five years. They were doing a great job and the church was strong so when they called us in to tell us that God had been speaking to them about their future, that He was calling them on, we were a bit surprised. They said, "We are moving on and we are putting the oversight of the church, the reins into your hands."

Timing is an interesting thing isn't it? For us, well mainly me, if they had given us this news any year previous to this year, we would have jumped at this opportunity. In my mind, (I emphasise, my mind only), I was always thinking, we could run a church, God give us a church. I think we should be pastors of a church. But never was that offered to us, and at times I couldn't understand why. I'd ask God the why question, but He would always remain silent on the matter.

Of course He had good reason for this. However at the time, I couldn't understand why He didn't at least give me some indication that He'd heard my prayer. I thought, maybe He just wants me to be patient and we would indeed have a church one day. Surely this had to be, it seemed the natural progression for us.

The truth is, He had not been ignoring me, He was simply waiting for me to be silent. I had been so busy telling Him, "Give us a church, give us church," that God had no room to speak. He couldn't get a word in edgeways. Good thing our God is a God of grace, mercy and lots of patience. However I am sure He was thinking, "Deb, when you're done, we can start chatting about My purposes for you."

The reason God had stayed so deafeningly quiet throughout those times I tried to tell Him what to do, was not only because I hadn't given Him space to talk, but because He wanted us to come to the place of realising being pastors of a local church was not our call, missions was. For us to reach the unreached in a nation not our own! Those mission seeds that had been planted deep inside of us many years ago had somehow become buried under the guise of what we were doing locally. The deeper we planted ourselves in this state, the more our focus was on the local church and community.

There is absolutely nothing wrong with being called to the local church. In fact, Paul and I take our hats off to pastors of local churches. We think those of you who are pastoring have the tougher gig. However, I have learnt over the years that when you have a mantle of something on you for a specific call, you can always think the other person's call is more difficult than your own. But when you are right in the centre of God's will for your life there is such a satisfaction, a sense of fulfillment that it makes you believe everyone would want to do what you're doing. Everyone would want to be a missionary. Who wouldn't want to sit in villages in the heat, humidity or the torrential rain, learn a new language and immerse yourself into a strange culture.

I'm in, how about you?

Well, it seems it's not everybody, because after being in Vietnam for several years, we had pastors come visit us saying, "Man, you have to be called to come to this place! Good on you Paul and Deb. There is no way I could do it." We would always respond by saying "Are you kidding me? This place is wonderful, we love it. We're swimming in this call of ours."

Was it easy? No. Calling doesn't equate to easy, but it definitely has to sit right and it did for us.

When a call is right you will know it. Will life be a breeze? Definitely not! If you want a non-eventful, risk free life, stay at home, lock your doors and don't leave your house. Stay safe. But God hasn't called us to easy or safe. He has called us to push the boundaries, to take risks and to be influencers who will leave a mark on this planet. Saying YES, even when it is uncomfortable, will do more for you than your no can possibly ever accomplish. So come on, step up to the plate and say YES. If I think of how our life would have been had we not taken the giant YES step to go to Tasmania that would eventually lead us to Vietnam, we would have missed out on so much. We would have missed knowing the countless people from all around the world with whom we have great relationships, the experiences that have seen us stand before prominent influential people, missed out on the opportunity of playing a part in seeing the national church gain recognition and so much more that would take a whole other book to tell you about. Saying YES is definitely better than safe and mundane!

When you make the choice to stay in God's wheelbarrow, you will be in for the ride of your life. Throughout your journey you will experience God on a whole other level. You will know His faithfulness when having to believe for the impossible. You will see His hand move mightily as He brings your breakthrough in times you think you have hit a

> Seriously, don't stay safe. Unlock your front door, step outside and let the sun shine on your face because there is a world out there to be won and a life to be lived to the full.

brick wall. You will experience His power as He opens doors for you that no man can shut. You will believe in His wealth of provision as He delivers into your hands everything you need. Seriously it's worth saying YES to God. Don't stay safe. Unlock your front door, step outside and let the sun shine on your face because there is a world out there to be won and a life to be lived to the full.

In the sixth year of serving in Tasmania, the reins of the church were handed to us, but by now God had maneuvered our hearts back to where He had first placed them, cross culturally. For us, this meant the church in our hands, was a temporary thing even though we were asked by many in the congregation to take it on fulltime. "Why don't you just take it on? You know the church. You have been doing so much in the church already, it makes sense and you would be good at it."

Those words of endorsement were nice, but no, we would not have been good at it. Yes, we could do it, but I don't believe we would have seen the church built to its full potential as it was purposed to be because that mantle was not on us. As a temporary measure, sure, we could carry it but to stay longer than was intended would be wrong. Wrong for the church, the congregation, ourselves and to the place and people we were really meant to pastor. Our true calling had regained clarity, we were ready to step into it.

So why would God send us to a place that had nothing to do with foreign missions if foreign missions was our calling? Why send us to be planted in a local church, serving it, growing to love the people there, being focused and putting all our energy into a place for six years, that was ultimately not to be where we put long-term roots down?

Glad you asked!

What we have come to know about God is this. God never makes mistakes. He is a multilevel, multipurpose God and what may seem out of left field to you and I, is actually at centre pitch to Him. When He called us to Tasmania to serve in the local church, He had a much bigger agenda in mind and that agenda was us! He needed to work on us and it obviously took Him six years. My goodness, I am so glad we weren't born in Moses' era. I don't think I could have done forty years. Yay for us that we got it a little quicker than that! God cracked us, molded us, shaped us, formed us, prepared us, armoured us, and blessed us in just six short years. Thank God.

10
MORE THAN ENOUGH

With the call now refueled and a heart ready to go, one question remained, "How was this all going to happen?" Changing states was a little different to moving countries! After six years of what seemed a diversion from our call (which actually wasn't, as I said), we were now about to embark on the journey of a lifetime, literally, but how was this all going to happen? We had the vision but no money as our financial situation had not changed. We knew very well the cost of moving from one state to the next, so moving countries was going to cost so much more. When we moved from Newcastle to Tasmania we had more than enough after the sale of our house and business but now God was saying move country with no resource!

We could have let our circumstances overwhelm us but we knew that if God was truly calling us and He was, He was definitely working out the logistics on our behalf. This we could rely on but again, for God to do what He needed to do we had to put James 2:22 into action.

If we were to take our family to this unknown territory, we needed to spy out the land, so we began to plan a 'taste and see' visit.

It was decided to make this a church mission trip so four others from the congregation joined us in this venture, and because Paul had been once, he was classed as the 'experienced one' and duly appointed leader. As the mighty trailblazer, he had to be the one who encouraged everyone to believe that God would provide. He kept up momentum, driving us all to trust in Jehovah Jireh who would prove Himself faithful for everything to come together. For our family, this meant trusting for not only one airfare and expenses but for all four of us.

Over a period of several months we met together to pray, encourage each other and continue planning our trip.

I remember one night, just six weeks out from leaving and Paul asked the usual opening question to our team, "How is everyone going with preparations and finance?"

I am so blessed to be married to such an incredible man of faith. When something gets in his spirit that God has spoken to him about, that's it for him. Nothing shakes him. It's a done deal. I have learnt a lot about faith from Paul. You know when you get asked that question, "Who has influenced you the most in your life apart from Jesus?" The first person I think of is my husband. Whenever I think of Paul's character, I think of a man with unwavering faith. God knew what He was doing when He put us together.

When Paul asked that question of the four who were coming with us, each one excitedly shared of the faithful provision of God. We were thrilled for them but our turn was coming. That same question was about to be posed to us, the ones leading the team. Team member Judy was the one to ask, "So, what about you guys, how is your finance going?" We really didn't want to answer that question but without any hesitation, my full of faith husband in his usual confident way smiled and said, "Well, we have $167."

Yes, that's right! Six weeks out and we had $167. You can imagine the look on our fellow travellers faces. "Really, you have only $167!" There was silence in the room that seemed to last forever, but in reality was less than a minute when one of the team piped up and said, "Well, we had better pray for you guys." Now there's an idea!! Up until this point our family had been praying our little hearts out for this trip but now after the team hearing this news, they wanted to get down in the dirt with us, with hands in the air, to petition heaven. "God, you hear that! We need a breakthrough now!" I looked over to Paul as we were praying and there he was, so at peace about it all. "God I so want that same peace in my spirit!"

On the way home in the car I said to Paul, "Aren't you worried?" And his answer was no surprise, "No, why should I be worried? God spoke so it's settled." I said, "Paul, I don't think I can believe for this trip, I am going to have to go on your faith." And being the loving, gentle, caring, encouraging husband he is, he said "Get your own faith, you can't have mine."

He had said it in a joking manner, but he was totally serious about it at the same time. You see, what he was saying to me was, "You can't go on my faith. You must believe God for yourself. You need to get with God and get that same conviction in your own spirit." Although it was not the answer I was looking for, it was the best thing he could have said to me. I really did need to get my own faith on this. I could not live my faith life through Paul or anyone else for that matter.

When a new challenge comes our way, we cannot lean on another's faith to grow ourselves in trusting God. We have to get that personal conviction in our own spirit to build what is called unshakable faith!

Over the next week, I spent some serious time with God asking Him to show me how He was going to provide such a great amount of money in such a short period of time. I had been in this place before. You know that place! The place where you just have to get before God completely undone, vulnerable and totally surrendered. Those raw meetings where it is just you and Him, pressing in, for as long as it takes, until there is a breakthrough and something drops into your spirit from heaven and you say, "That's it!"

I know, without a shadow of a doubt, that God wants us all to come to the place where we meet Him beyond the veil, beyond that curtain where we dare to step into His inner sanctuary known as God's holy of holies, the place where everything makes sense. It is here we become reacquainted with the unencumbered, unrestricted One, He who is all mighty, all knowing, all possible and is called Abba Father.

How unfortunate it is though, for many of us, that only in times of challenge, heartache or confusion do we turn back to this place of intimacy with our Father God. Can you imagine how different our daily walk would be if we had the conviction, "If God be for us, who can be against us." Romans 8:31 (NIV)

It took several days sitting in God's throne room before breakthrough came one morning. I did as I had every day, took my Bible, and went and sat down on the back steps of our house. With the sun shining in my face, I simply flipped open the book at a random page with the hope that somehow, this page, would hold the answer I was looking for.

I know when we are baby Christians, flipping open the Bible works because God wants to make it as easy as possible for babies to grow but once we become more mature, He expects us to be more purposeful in seeking His face. However, in saying this, I do believe there are occasions He wants to help us out just because, and this was a 'just because' moment from Him to me.

As the pages fell open to Genesis 41, I began to read about the plight of Joseph, the pain he'd been through, the captivity, the wrongful accusations and disappointment but as I continued reading, my eyes fell upon verse 52, where for both Joseph and myself, came God's saving grace. It was my revelation moment of how God was going to do the impossible for us. Verse 52, Joseph names his second son Ephraim because he said, "God has made me fruitful in this land of my grief." (NLT)
WOW! God could bless me, in the land of my grief.

Those words jumped right off the page and into my lap. I cannot describe clearly enough of how powerful this verse was to me that day, "God has made me fruitful in this land of my grief." Gen 41:52 (NLT)

I said "Oh God - the business! The business we bought, that has robbed us of everything, has been our land of suffering, of our grief for so long but somehow, You God are going to use it to bless us. The revelation was so strong in my spirit it was like someone had hit me with a defibrillator and I had come alive again full of faith. In the natural it was insane to think that the very thing that caused us pain could be the source of blessing for us to get to Vietnam but God had spoken and He could make dry bones live.

What happened over the next six weeks was nothing short of a miracle. Business came flowing through the door like never before. Up until this point, no matter what Paul tried to do to make sales and build clientele in order to generate income, it would always come to naught, yet during this season, business began to pour in. Never had we seen anything like this in all the time we had had the business. It happened just like when Jesus instructed his disciples when catching fish.

> When he finished teaching, he said to Simon, "Push out into deep water and let your nets out for a catch." Simon said, "Master, we've been fishing hard all night and haven't caught even a minnow. But if you say so, I'll let out the nets." It was no sooner said than done - a huge haul of fish, straining the nets past capacity. They waved to their partners in the other boat to come help them. They filled both boats, nearly swamping them with the catch.
>
> Luke 5:4-7 (MSG)

Paul cast out his net once again and watched, as it began to fill to capacity.

We needed $11,000 and over that six-week period a profit of $9,000 was made through our business. During this time, we also received a letter from our insurance company saying they were restructuring the company and the insurance bonuses could be taken as shares or cashed in. Ours added up to $3,000 so of course we cashed them in.

Now we not only had the $11,000 we needed but an extra $1,000 bonus amount. Our net had been filled past capacity!

Try as we might, we had not been able to find anyone who could lend us a video camera to capture every day's activities during the upcoming missions trip to show the church upon our return. Now, we had enough money to buy our own camera! That night just a few weeks earlier, as we and our team knelt at God's feet, we could not have imagined in our wildest dreams what He had planned to do. It has been nothing short of a miracle.

Ephesians 3:20 (NIV) is true, "Now to him who is able to do immeasurably more than all we ask or imagine, according to his power that is at work within us."

Paul was so excited about the turn around in the business. He thought God had finally pulled out the plug from the dam and it would be all systems go from here on in, but that was not meant to be.

After we had all that we needed, the door again shut on the business. It was so black and white. God had opened the floodgate and poured out all we needed, then shut it just as tight as it was before. Paul pleaded with God to continue to keep this door open, but God spoke very clearly to him saying, "You have all you need."

We knew God had us in the school of learning to trust Him in a deeper way, but sometimes we weren't thrilled with His methods, and so tried to push the envelope a little further.

I cannot emphasis strongly enough to you that as you journey with God, you can fully depend, rely, trust, rest, lean on, believe in His, 'more than enough' for you. The future He has for you is guaranteed and He will remain faithful and fully committed your whole journey. His unseen plan that He already laid out for you, way before you were even born, is in place and waiting for you. That is not the issue. The issue is you. You, believing and walking in what is already set up! He waits patiently for you to rise up and begin your, one step in front of the other adventure, with Him. He waits for you to say those words that will change your destiny. YES I will!

His ability to bring everything He has for you to pass is sure. Don't wait any longer, because you owe it to yourself and everyone waiting in the wings who God has ordained you to pour your life out for. You are the only you God has, and ever will create, and it is you and you alone who can fulfill your destiny.

11
HERE WE GO!

The alarm goes off, the date is the 16th January, 1997 and it's 3:50am. We can hardly contain our excitement. Paul and I get up, have our showers and are dressed in no time and unlike a school day, Belinda and Josh were already up and dressed ready for this exciting adventure. The doorbell rings and our fabulous, 'get up early for no other reason other that to take us to the airport' friends, are standing at our front door, ready to be of service.

When we arrived at the airport the rest of our team were already there, eagerly waiting for us. On entering the terminal, we were greeted by many people from the church who had decided to get up at this unearthly hour of the morning to pray with us and see us off. Amazing! In front of this fan club of ours, stood an enormous banner they had made which read "Liberty Assembly Of God Bridging the Gap" and under those words were each of our names. "Bridging the Gap." Yes, this is exactly want we intended to do when we got to Vietnam. Bridge the gap by showing God's love in action, meeting people at their point of need, and then by doing this, earn the right to speak life into their lives.

On seeing all our beautiful church people at the airport that morning, I thought to myself, "What an amazing church we have." It spoke so loud of how they'd truly taken ownership of this mission trip, even though not all were physically able to come with us. That's family right there!

These days flying is almost like catching a bus. Travel is so much more accessible and affordable than ever before with more direct routes, making flying time even quicker. You can leave home in the morning and be anywhere in the world within twenty-four hours. In 1997 there were no direct flights from Australia to Vietnam which meant we not only had to fly from the island state of Tasmania to the mainland of Australia, we also had to take several detours via other Asian nations to get to our destination.

We knew it was going to be a long journey but we were all so pumped and motivated, we didn't care how long it took, we were up for it.

Apart from Paul, this was going to be our team's first experience of Asia, so along with excitement, came a little apprehension as to how we would go with the process of getting through immigration and customs. We were all very aware that Vietnam had not long opened its doors to the west and any visitors coming in were still viewed with some suspicion.

Before reaching Vietnam, we had a stopover in the nation of Thailand. Was this country going to be as dubious about visitors? We had been travelling all day from early morning and tiredness was starting to set in. All we wanted to do was get through immigration and customs without a hitch, get into a taxi and to our hotel so we could put our head on a real pillow and go to sleep.

Thai immigration was a nice surprise. With a quick glance at our faces to make sure we matched our passport photos, they stamped a visa stamp in our passports and waved us through. Step one done. Although we had breezed through immigration it was not over yet. We collected our bags from the carousel and headed to the customs counter. It was here we got a little apprehensive because we were carrying in lots of equipment for the project we were going to be doing and some of the items we had were hard to explain what they were for (How do you explain a big metal flying fox track to someone who has no reference to what that is?). Would they want to open every case and ask questions about each item? Would this be a long in-depth discussion of why we were carrying these big metal objects? One by one we put our cases on the belt to be scanned waiting for the dreaded voice saying, "Wait, what is this?" But nothing. Not even an enquiring eye. Customs also was a breeze. We all breathed a huge sigh of relief and confidently walked out of the airport. From now on we could relax, because all we had to do now was hail a taxi and get to the hotel. A piece of cake right?

Ha! We soon learnt we weren't in Kansas anymore, Dorothy!

Haggling with the taxis turned out to be a nightmare, a real nightmare! We decided to split up into two groups of four to make it easy due to having so many bags. Every time we attempted to get into a taxi that pulled up in front of us someone would push us out the way, hop in the taxi and close the door before we had a chance to say, "Hey, that was my taxi." Other taxis would take one look at us all with our mountain of bags and drive straight past us. This happened over and over again. We felt like we were fighting a loosing battle and after what seemed like hours but in reality was probably about forty-five minutes, one did agree to stop and take us. He hailed a second taxi and we all cheered. Finally, we were going to get out of here. They asked us where we were going in their broken English and we pointed to what was like scribble to us, the Thai address. We weren't really sure they understood but our driver was nodding and putting our bags in the boot so we believed everyone understood each other. Once our bags were in the boot (which didn't close by the way), the drivers decided they didn't want to take us after all and took all our bags out again. By this time our excitement had turned to complete frustration and I was thinking, "I don't like this place. I'm tired, it's hot and these people are rude."

In our exasperation, we decided we needed God's help or we would never get out of the airport, so we sent up a quick prayer and the moment we said amen, Paul spotted a mini van. He asked the driver if he could take us to our hotel and like music to our ears in perfect English he said. "Yes, ok no problem!!" Thank God. We piled in, bags and all, and this time we really were on our way to the hotel.

That was our first acquaintance with cross culture stress and somehow I sensed it was not going to be the last.

It was good to wake the next morning refreshed after a full night's sleep and a delicious breakfast consisting of French toast with maple syrup, bacon, fresh fruit, tea and coffee. A decent sleep and good food made the previous night's drama fade into a distant memory.

There was still time before we had to leave for our flight to Vietnam so we went up to the top floor balcony of the hotel to enjoy the view. As we sat overlooking the countless Thai rooftops, I couldn't help but think how different this place was to where we lived. As I got lost in my own thoughts, I sensed the presence of the Holy Spirit come upon me and in that moment, felt completeness. This was where I belong, where our family belongs. I didn't want to be anywhere else. Already, Asia had begun to capture my spirit and yet I was still to realise that one day, it would become my heartland.

It had been two years since Paul's first trip to Vietnam and from that time until now, he did his best to prepare our family for this trip. From the videos and photos he took and stories he told, he shared of its magnificent scenery and the lifestyle in all its extremes. He talked about the strange and unfamiliar smells that wafted through the air as people cooked in makeshift kitchens in their homes or on the street. He also spoke of the unimaginable traffic that relentlessly flowed like a river twenty-four hours a day, and how he learnt to negotiate the ebbs and flow of it in order to cross to the other side of the street. We had taken it all in, listening to every word, creating a picture in our mind of his every experience with the Vietnamese people, over and over again. Now it was our turn to bathe in this wonderful culture. I was so ready for this, and just wanted to be there.

Getting through Vietnam immigration and customs was surprisingly easy, and seeing our hosts waiting on the other side of the barrier was a welcomed sight. They even had a van ready waiting for us. Yay no taxi hassles!

The hour-long trip from the airport to the hotel was nothing short of fascinating. It was everything Paul had described and more. As we drove past numerous rice paddies dotted with families planting their crops or leading buffaloes across their fields, it made me realise just how far removed our life was from theirs. The roads were so different as we experienced continual near misses from the chaotic swerving trucks, buses, cars, motorbikes and bicycles, each one clamoring for position on the narrow two lane roads. I couldn't get enough of it and our kids were wide eyed trying to take in everything that was happening around them. I just wanted to get to the hotel so we could check in and step out amongst it all.

After arriving at the hotel and putting our gear in our room, the wait for the rest of our team to join us seemed like an eternity. I just wanted to go and go now!!! I was so sure I was up for anything, every sight, every sound and even every unusual smell. I was ready, totally prepared! Nothing was going to rattle this chickadee! Come on team, let's go. Let's just go!

Finally we got to step out into the world of Vietnam and it was wonderful. Every sight, every smell, every sound was nothing short of exhilarating. This place was so incredibly alive. Children playing on the streets were completely unfazed by the traffic swerving around them. Vendors were going about their daily routine, selling anything and everything to earn a day's wage yet wore the biggest smiles I had ever seen. The sound of horns from motorbikes or tinkling of bells from bicycles constantly ringing to say, "We're passing," was the music of the city. I was in love with it all and wanted to bottle it up so I could take it with me wherever I went.

I was so taken up with these new sights and sounds that I hadn't noticed at first, other people who were also part of this landscape. They were everywhere. I saw them, but all of a sudden, I was now seeing them.

They were the beggars and the homeless. The nameless faces of society, both young and old, lining the sidewalk and sleeping in doorways. All of a sudden I found myself in a mind spin. I had come face-to-face with this other reality and everything inside me screamed, "No, no, no, this is not right! This is not fair!" I had very quickly gone from exuberance to being incredibly overwhelmed with grief and stress at what I was now noticing. "They don't have anywhere safe to lay their head. They have no place to call their own."

These people were the outcasts, the lost, the broken and I was helpless to do anything about it. I said, "Paul, take me back to the hotel, I can't handle this." "But Deb, I told you about this. I told you this is what you would see. You saw the photos and video. You knew you would come face-to-face with this." "I know Paul, but now it is real, now I am touching it and I can't deal with this right now."

I had no idea I would react this way. There was no warning sign, it just happened, and right then and there I had to get out immediately.

Paul was gracious enough to take the kids and me straight back to the hotel so I could calm down from the overwhelming culture stress I was going through and process my feelings. I knew that if I didn't do this, I could not face going out on those streets again. I definitely did not come all this way to be defeated by a culture stress moment caused by this new world. I had to deal with it.

Thank God, morning bought a new perspective on things. It's amazing how daylight makes everything look so different. My confidence had returned and I once again ventured out into this new culture I had committed to being part of for the next month.

There is something about light that makes everything right, everything clear. I remember once as a child, learning this very lesson. I had jumped into bed and after reading my favorite book for the second or third time, I turned off the light but as I began closing my eyes I glanced up to see sitting on top of my wardrobe an enormous frog. I didn't know where it came from, but it made me feel very scared. I was so scared in fact, that

I didn't move a muscle. I didn't even want to turn the light back on for fear it would pounce on me. Its clear dark form was so overwhelming I could not sleep but inevitably as the night wore on, I felt my eyes getting heavier and heavier. Try as I might, I knew I could not stay awake any longer so I ever so slowly pulled the sheets over my head and prayed for God to please protect me from this big bad frog who had entered my bedroom uninvited. As morning came and the light shone into my room, I found that the gigantic frog that had frozen me with fear half the night was nothing more than a pile of clothing that had been left unfolded on top of the wardrobe.

I can laugh about it now, but at the time it was real, it was frightening and I felt helpless to do anything about it.

Whether your fear is warranted or not, you have to face it and deal with it. You have to process it and move on or you too will find yourself frozen in time. More often than not, you will find that your big bad frog ends up being just a pile of unfolded clothing on top of your wardrobe. But even if it's not, there is always an answer, always a solution.

John 1:5 (NIV) tells us, "The light shines in the darkness, and the darkness has not overcome it."

We have a Saviour, His name is Jesus Christ and He has the ability to dispel all darkness from any place in our life. If He could do it for me, He could do it for those beggars and homeless that we'd met on the street that previous night and for every other beggar, homeless, abused, abandoned and devalued person on this earth. The God of more than enough has chosen you and me to be the ones to bring them out of these dark places into His light that brings with it hope, destiny, purpose and love.

For Paul and me, one of our biggest highlights was watching our kids, Belinda and Josh take on every challenge that was put before them. Whether that was climbing down mountain ranges, befriending children who were covered in scabies, dealing with the proverbial 'Asian Trots' or working with primitive equipment (including using scissors to cut grass) in the heat, to building a playground for blind children. The Asian trots were probably one of our biggest challenges in Vietnam. In those days, the country was still quite undeveloped, so to find ourselves suffering from food poisoning of some form or another was not unexpected. It hit most of us at some point throughout our trip and I sensed it was my turn as we headed to the station to catch the train from Hanoi down to Da Nang. To say that our seventeen- hour trip was a memorable one would be an understatement. No sooner had we found our cabin, it hit me. While our team enjoyed views of rice fields and village scenes from their comfortable cabin I was to enjoy a more interesting landscape in the shape of a not so clean, metal toilet bowl. I was confined to the moving bathroom for those long seventeen hours and although the story of my relationship with that squat toilet would be graphically interesting, I will spare you the details leaving it to your imagination.

By the time we reached Da Nang I was tired, drained, in pain, shivering and all I wanted to do right there and then was curl up in my own comfortable bed that was dressed with clean sheets and a soft pillow. This was not going to happen. In vast contrast, we were stepping off a train into yet another unfamiliar city to be greeted by thousands of Asian people who lined the platform waiting for their loved ones to disembark or they themselves, to get on board for their desired destination. Among the sea of Asian faces, a white face appeared. It was our host. He pushed through the crowd to meet us as we stepped off the train and his friendly smile was comforting to see. This patient host who had stood waiting on the platform of Da Nang Station for several hours due to the late arrival of our train was equally as happy to see us. As he greeted each one of us, he asked us one at a time, how we were enjoying Vietnam. I had hoped he would skip me because I could not give him a positive response. Our team, on the other hand, were more than happy to share their stories and experiences including the novel train trip they had just taken. But for me, try as I might, I couldn't think of any 'wow' moments at that point. I just looked at our host and smiled politely, not saying a word but inside I was thinking, "I don't like it and I'm not coming back here again."

Don't you just love God's sense of humor? I am sure He was having a huge belly laugh as I said those words in my mind that day and at the same time saying, "Deb, you have no idea right now, but very soon, you are not only going to come back to this place, but you will pour your heart and life out for it."

If God laid out our whole future in front of us including the ups and downs of it all, how many of us would actually say YES to Him. YES, I am up for that. Count me in God, no matter what! I think I could safely say not many. God has very good reason to only give us bite size pieces of our puzzle. He knows how much we can handle at one time. If we did know it all from beginning to end, we would freak out at the enormity of it or even say, "God, I think you have the wrong person." On the other end of the spectrum, dare I say, some of us may start to get a swelled head believing it's because we are so wonderful and that is why He has chosen us. Just be satisfied with how much He chooses to reveal to you at any one time and go along with His plan. It's for your good and for His glory!

Whose glory is it for anyway?

One year later, I remember God speaking to me very clearly just before leaving Australia again for Vietnam. He said, "Deb, what if you don't get recognised or receive any glory for what you do in Vietnam?" At that time it was easy to say, "No problem," to God, because we had not done anything yet. We had not poured out our lives, nor built anything significant that would warrant any glory, but after eighteen years of sowing much and seeing something established in Vietnam, can I say, "No problem" as easily now?

If we are all honest with ourselves, we want to receive some recognition and some glory. I am not saying we should not recognise, encourage and appreciate achievements but what I am saying is, it is not us who sits on the throne. God must stay on the throne in our lives, in our ministries, in our successes. I am very conscious of those words He spoke to me that day and my heart is for Him to be glorified in all that has been achieved here. It must remain all about Him.

After getting off that train and into a comfortable bed for a few days, I regained a fresh perspective on Vietnam. Those few days of rest saw both my hunger and eagerness return.

The next two weeks went as planned. We build a specialised playground in a school for around one hundred blind students. Although this playground was going to be a huge blessing for them, we had a sense that this whole exercise was going to do more in us.

It was the simple things that began to change us. For one, the appreciation of the labour saving devices we had in Australia as we began cutting the grass with scissors and using prehistoric shovels that needed daily repairing to dig holes for poles and also learning to be grateful for the unrecognisable food that we received every day, lovingly prepared by the teachers who personally went to the market to choose the best produce so we would not get sick. Our hearts were growing warmer towards these beautiful people and their country as we got to know a culture that freely opens its heart to welcome in strangers as their own. Even the noise of the traffic and tropical heat was no longer intruding in on our space. God was doing a number on us.

One of the many wonderful things about the Vietnamese people is they are so easy to connect with. They sincerely want to be your friend. They take you into their heart and you become like family instantly. This happened when first meeting Cau and his family back in 1997. Cau, a man who stepped out of his shop one day in 1995 to help a lost westerner looking for the way back to his hotel. That westerner was the very first AOG World Relief worker who came for a short time with his family to get something started here in Da Nang through our missions organisation. As Tony stood looking dazed at a map of the city near Cau's shop, without hesitation Cau, jumped to his aid. A chance meeting you may say? Definitely not! In the plans of God, Tony was meant to stand exactly in front of Cau's shop that day. He could have been standing only metres to the left or to the right of this shop, but God had purposed Tony to stand right in front of a shop in order to take its owner, Cau, on a brand new future, a pathway that would fulfill his destiny, planned long ago in God's mind. And as the saying goes, our long association with our amazing Cau is history.

But I cannot leave it there. I have to tell you one more thing about our friend, our colleague, our brother, our Cau. Cau is a man who has a heart much bigger than his stature. A man who in 1997, was willing to put aside his own needs for the sake of others. A man who would choose to close his small hardware shop at the drop of a hat to do whatever was needed to be done in order to help us help his people. Closing his shop meant loss of income for him and his family. What he earned in one day would barely provide enough to feed them for that day, and yet he chose to sacrificially give of his time and effort despite his own personal circumstances. How humbling this was to us, knowing this. We were incredibly grateful for his help, but felt guilty that he would be so self-sacrificing. We would say "Cau, you need to work" but he insisted on helping us, saying, "You are helping my people, I must help you."

Without a doubt in my mind, I know God has been smiling on Cau all his life. God loves and honors those who are sold out for others. Unknowingly at the time, Cau was practicing the very commandment that Jesus gave us in John 13:34 (NIV) "Love one another as I have loved you." Cau was definitely doing that and God blesses him and his family in incredible and miraculous ways for it.

When we live with an open, honest, right motivated heart, God smiles on us. When we abandon ourselves to Him and trust in Him fully, He will always prove to us that He is a well that never runs dry. It is a very real lesson that reveals the true nature of God. He is a giver, not a taker.

> When we abandon ourselves to Him and trust in Him fully, He will always prove to us that He is a well that never runs dry.

Cau's family and ours bonded straight away, a bond that would see us joined together in service to God and commitment to each other all our life. In 1997 however, after our work was completed in Da Nang and we boarded the train to leave there was a sadness left behind as we waved goodbye to each other not knowing whether we would ever meet again.

In just a short four weeks, our family and team laboured in heat, met with the unusual, experienced the uncomfortable and got violently ill, but that paled into insignificance as we gained new perspective on culture, joined hearts with a new nation and were challenged for the future. Now our footprints were imbedded deep within their soil.

Our return trip to Australia took us through the country of Singapore. We only stayed one night but it was a night that was to shake me just as much as when we walked down the streets of Hanoi that first evening. No longer was I seeing poverty, lack and hopelessness, but a country with abundance and wealth with its spotlessly clean streets. A country that had everything, but was seemingly oblivious to their next door neighbour's plight. Again, everything within me screamed, this is not fair!

We walked into McDonalds and every table was full. Full of Singaporeans who looked healthy and strong, and in my mind, had more on their plate than they needed. I could only think of the Vietnamese who struggled to put anything on their table from one day to the next, while this nearby country was abundant in wealth. I was angry. I was angry that they could have so much while their Asian neighbours had so little. I couldn't stand it. We ate and then we left. Once again I needed to process my feelings.

There is a danger when going cross culturally for a short season, spending time with people who seemingly have nothing, immersing yourself emotionally in their world. You can find you are left feeling indignant, angry or even want to start a campaign to change what doesn't seem right. While all this may seem good or justified, it doesn't necessarily mean our intentions are going to make a difference until we take time to process the realities of their life and find out what would be best for them long term.

You see, for those who are living in a developing world, we need to remember these people are all developing together. Yes, they want a better life, but we who have more than enough, feel more pity for them, than they do for themselves, and it is easy to throw out a Band Aid solution to make it better. We need to take the time to get into their shoes to see what they really need or we could actually make things worse.

12
THE ISSUE OF DOUBT AND FEAR

Returning to Aussie soil was both bitter sweet and surreal for me. What just happened? This was my first thought as clean paved paths, tarred roads, modern cars and shopping centres stood before me. The world we had just left now seemed so far away as this all so familiar world invaded my being once again. What now God, now that we have had this earth shaking, life changing experience?

"Don't get too comfortable about your future. If you are not unsettled already, He is going to come and unsettle you and release you into another dimension of the call of God. A great requirement is coming upon you and your lives."

Just eight weeks after arriving home, this was the prophetic word spoken over us from yet another visiting speaker at church. This time the word was a little more palatable on the heart than the one we had received when first arriving in Tassie!

We were not only feeling unsettled, but restless, knowing there was more on the horizon for us and that it was coming quickly, and over that horizon was Vietnam. We had said YES to God when we moved our whole family from Newcastle to Tasmania. We had said YES to God when he told Paul to go on the very first trip to Vietnam. We had said YES to God when we took our family on our exploratory trip there and now we were about to say YES to God for a life of service in that foreign land. Could we do this?

We still had numerous mountains to climb. There were still bills to be paid, a business to come out from under which still had its tentacles gripping us, and family adjustments to be made. What on earth is the first step? God what do we do? And God answered very clearly, "Speak. I want you to speak it out, speak it into existence."

Speak it out. You can sit around waiting for something to happen, someone to do something or say something to you, lightning to strike you three times as a sign, for that magic green light to shine on you or you can just do what God expects you to do and put James 2:22 into action. If you choose the former, you already know the answer. I have said numerous times before, you will be sitting, waiting for a very long time. God only works with moving vehicles and the first station platform you need to step onto is the 'Speak it Out' platform.

For us, even without the prophesy, we knew there was a new stirring in our heart that something greater was coming and James 2:22 had to be put into gear.

I believe Jonathan is the perfect example for us to follow when it comes to putting legs on our faith.

> One day Jonathan son of Saul said to his young armor-bearer, "Come, let's go over to the Philistine outpost on the other side." But he did not tell his father. Saul was staying on the outskirts of Gibeah under a pomegranate tree in Migron. With him were about six hundred men, among whom was Ahijah, who was wearing an ephod. He was a son of Ichabod's brother Ahitub son of Phinehas,

> the son of Eli, the Lord's priest in Shiloh. No one was aware that Jonathan had left. On each side of the pass that Jonathan intended to cross to reach the Philistine outpost was a cliff; one was called Bozez and the other Seneh. One cliff stood to the north toward Mikmash, the other to the south toward Geba. Jonathan said to his young armor-bearer, "Come, let's go over to the outpost of those uncircumcised men. Perhaps the Lord will act in our behalf. Nothing can hinder the Lord from saving, whether by many or by few."
>
> 1 Samuel 14:1 -6 (NIV)

For too long Saul and his men had sat, and sat, and sat, waiting for the right time, but they missed it. All the while, Jonathan was willing to believe God would be with him in defeating his enemies. He moved forward, and each step of the way, said to God, this is what I think we are to do, "You stop me, change my direction if I am wrong."

If you take a moment to read the whole passage, you will see Jonathan defeated what seemed an impossible enemy with not six hundred men, but with just his armour bearer and God on his side. By the time Saul decided to do something, it was all over.

Jonathan spoke it out, "Let's go."

> "Do all that you have in mind," his armor-bearer said. "Go ahead; I am with you, heart and soul." Jonathan said, "Come then; we will cross over toward the men and let them see us. If they say to us, 'Wait there until we come to you,' we will stay where we are and not go up to them. But if they say, 'Come up to us,' we will climb up, because that will be our sign that the LORD has given them into our hands."
>
> 1 Samuel 14:7 - 10 (NIV)

What is holding you back? Are you still sitting under that pomegranate tree? Don't you think you have been sitting under there long enough? Do what the lyrics in the movie Frozen says to do "Let it go, let it go." Are you frozen? Frozen in your tracks like Saul was, or will you be like

Jonathon and say, "Ok, that's enough sitting around. Let's go and do what we are meant to do."

So we spoke it out. "Guess what everyone, God is calling us to Vietnam!" There, we said it. We took the first step and spoke it out. What a release in our spirit that was, and to our surprise, the response from people was overwhelming. "Yes, we see that. It's all over you, we are with you on this."

You can work yourselves up about what people might think, what people will say, how people may oppose you, but guess what? Just maybe, there will be many who will say, as Jonathan's armour bearer did, "Do what you think is best, I am with you completely, whatever you decide." Of course there will be some who disagree with you, but don't let those nay-sayers stop you from your call or you could miss out on defeating the Philistines.

I assume you have got my point by now and have boarded the train of destiny for your life and if you have done that, well done!

As your train begins to move, what you will find is that the trip doesn't go as fast as you expected it to. You may wonder if you actually got on the right train. Let me remind you that there is an enemy who is not pleased with the decision you have made, so he tries to lead you to the station of doubt.

Our human nature defaults to doubt, and the enemy knows it. It's interesting how we can quote our many testimonies to people of the countless times God has come through for us and we praise Jesus for His amazing faithfulness, yet the next hurdle, the next challenge, request or faith steps we have to take, worries the socks off us! God then comes through for us in His usual style, and we again go into our 'praise God' routine until the next time something comes our way and we do that same old dance again.

So because our train seems to be going at a snail's pace, we find ourselves getting anxious. Are we going to get to where we need to go? Is it going to be on time? Will I have everything I need for where I am going? So many questions swirl around in our mind.

Well let me answer those questions for you, but first of all, I do want to encourage you once again by saying, "Good job for getting on the train." Secondly, I want to let you in on a little secret, you train catcher. You are in the minority. Yes, that's right, the minority. Many are called, but few are chosen. Many say, "Oh yes I want to do this for God or that for God," but you will find them still sitting at the train station watching all the trains of opportunities pass them by, all the while saying to themselves, "I'll catch the next one, the next will be the right one, the best timed one, the more secure one, the more convenient one." But, you brave and adventurous soul, you have said, "Hey, that's my train and I'm getting on it!"

Now to answer your doubt obstacle, let me ask you one question. When you got on that train, who did you think was your driver? Of course God! So relax and trust in how He gets you to your destination. Don't try and control the reins of how it all comes together because God is not unprepared, like we often are. In fact God has set everything up even before we call on Him.

Isaiah 65:24 (NLT) says "I will answer them before they even call to me. While they are still talking about their needs, I will go ahead and answer their prayers!"

> When doubt comes knocking at your door, let Isaiah 65:24 (NLT) answer it

That's security right there!
When doubt comes knocking at your door, let Isaiah 64:24 answer it.

I also love what Malachi 3:6 (NKJV) says, "For I am the Lord, I do not change; Therefore you are not consumed, O sons of Jacob." Firstly, God never changes and secondly, you and I will not be consumed. We don't need to be defeated by doubt or anything else that tries to hinder our journey.

Jonathon obviously believed in Malachi 3:6 because he refused to be consumed by insurmountable odds, obstacles or distractions.

- He had a 'rising up' spirit, willing to take a chance. (1 Samuel 14:1a)
- He chose carefully whom he conferred with, sharing only with faith filled, God trusting people. (1 Samuel 14:1b)
- He believed that although there were insurmountable obstacles before him, he could trust in his bigger God (1 Samuel 14:6)
- He was not prideful in his advance forward, but conferred with God along the way. (1 Samuel 14:8-11)
- He was active in the miracle (1 Samuel 14:13)

Those lessons from Jonathan really encouraged me as we faced our own hurdles. We still had to deal with numerous Philistine financial and business issues but we knew camping under the pomegranate tree was not going to slay these giants. Like Jonathon we chose to rise up, trust God, and become active in our miracle, and as we did this, we saw the Philistines crumble, one by one and our faith grew as strong as a rock.

I am so thankful that we didn't quit when obstacles and difficulties came hurtling at us during those six years in Tasmania because although we faced many challenges, there was a greater abundance of precious jewels God handed to us at each station He took us to. Precious jewels that continue to serve us well today, gems we would never have received, never would have learnt from had we got off the train at Doubt City or Too Hard Town.

On the scales of life, jewels far outweigh any obstacle that comes our way. The reality about obstacles and difficulties is, they are temporary, but jewels, they are keepers for a lifetime.

> On the scales of life, jewels far outweigh any obstacle. Obstacles are temporary, but jewels are precious keepers for a lifetime.

The sad part of Jonathon's story is Saul. Saul could have been the one to lead this victory, but he chose to stay put. In 1 Samuel 14:2 it says that Saul was camped, not just sitting. When we think of camping, we think of setting up, unpacking, relaxing, throwing away our watches and letting the day float by. That is a dangerous place to be when God is asking us to actively be involved in our miracle journey. Saul was not only camping with his six hundred men but the Bible specifically makes reference to Ichabod. In verse 3 it says that Ahijah was a son of Ichabod's brother, Ahitub, son of Phinehas, the son of Eli, the LORD's priest in Shiloh. The Bible could have just said Ahijah was the son of Ahitub and then explained the lineage, but it specifically mentions Ichabod. Why? Because Ichabod means departed glory. Saul was no longer under God's glory cloud because he had chosen to camp rather than be ready when his opportunity arose, but unfortunately God had already moved on.

Are you saying we shouldn't take a breather? No, rest periods are important, but God never intends for us to be camping when we are supposed to be packed ready to go. Stay under the glory cloud of God. Sit too long and the anointing will be passed on to someone who is willing to rise up.

My husband Paul, is always saying, serving God is both exciting and terrifying at the same time and he's right.

Let me tell you about my amazing, stable, level headed, unwavering, faith filled husband, Paul. He is a visionary, a mentor, a leader and as humble as they come. Yes, I got the whole package when God gave me Paul. We began dating when I was 16 and I can say without a shadow of doubt, he has always been an amazing faithful man in every way. Whatever we have been through, believed for, journeyed in, his faith and stability have always been steadfast. God is so good at putting opposites together, not that I am a total yoyo, but Paul has definitely bought balance to me in many ways. Now as we entered this new season, Paul in his predictable way, would stay incredibly relaxed about how it would all come together. If fear or doubt rose up in me, he would always answer, "Don't worry, God's got it all in hand."

When the angel Gabriel, visited both Zachariah and Mary with similar messages of miracle births (Luke 1:5-38 NLT), both felt fear and both had the same question for God's messenger, "How is this possible?" Yet one was chastised for disbelief and the other was not. Why?

We need to understand the difference between Zachariah's response and Mary's response. Both felt fear. However, this was not the issue. The unknown will always cause us to have a natural fear. Both asked, "How is this possible?" but again, the question alone was not the issue. God has no problem with us asking questions like that. The difference was trust. Total belief in what God has promised. Zachariah's "How is this possible?" challenged God to prove it, whereas Mary's, "How is this possible?" meant, "I don't understand, but I trust You."

This is the key for us if we are truly going to leave the safety of our comfort zone for the extraordinary life God has promised us. To be able to say, "Even though I don't know how it will be, I trust You."

Despite the different responses from both Mary and Zachariah, God did not say to Zachariah, "Well then, it's not going to happen for you, I'll find someone else." No, this was not a Saul 'camping under a tree' issue, but a doubting Thomas style 'prove it to me' comeback that Zachariah was putting before God. God did however need to teach him a lesson in trust, so he silenced him by taking away his ability to speak for a period of time to prove that what He had predicted would indeed come to pass.

We all have fear and doubt moments in our lives like Mary, even prove it God times like Zachariah, yet God still turns to us and says, "I choose you." The difference between Mary and Zachariah's experience though, was one got to enjoy the journey fully, while the other did not.

After God revealed to us that our world was about to be enlarged, I too, like Mary, asked the question of God, "But how is it possible, I trust You Lord, but how can it possibly be?"

Paul and I once again got on our knees before God and asked Him to prepare us for what was ahead. I then went and grabbed my journal and marked the day, 20th of September, 1997 and wrote diagonally across one whole page, "Our journey to Vietnam. For such a time as this, a journey of miracles."

After writing those words I then asked God if He would give us a piece of manna every day to guide and encourage us on this, our biggest journey in our lives so far.

"God will You, from this day, today, until the day we board that plane for Vietnam, show me something, anything, a word, a miracle, a sign every day, that says, Deb, you and your family are on the right track in this new venture, this is your destiny and you can trust me."

After praying that prayer, God took me on a personal two hundred day journey with Him during which I got to know God in all facets of His being. I would like to now take you on that journey to get a glimpse of how walking with God, seeing Him in the every day can bring you closer to Him. Come with me now on a brief tour of those two hundred amazing days as we shift gears.

Part 3: 200 Days Of Miracles

I am thrilled that you have decided to join me on this incredible journey and discover as I have, how deep and how wide our Father God truly is, to know how much He desires to bring us closer to Him and show us His unmatched power and authority working in our lives. For us, over those two hundred days, God did miracles, gave us words of revelation, provided from empty oil vessels, moved mountains and presented us before leaders.

My prayer for you, as you read these two hundred days, is that you put your own name, your own situation into each day and watch God work for you and in you so you too will grasp just how much He loves and cares for you beyond your wildest dreams.

Day 1   DON'T RISK YOUR DESTINY

It was day one of this two hundred day journey and I had no idea what nugget would fall from heaven but I was expectant, waiting on God to show up. I sat down with my cup of tea and opened up the Evangel Magazine, a church magazine that used to be sent out to all AOG churches. As I flipped it open it landed on a page that had an article titled in big black letters, 'Don't Risk Your Destiny.' The title almost knocked me over. As I began to read, these words in particular jumped out:

> Opposition, persecution and suffering cannot stop any life that is totally dedicated to the will and purpose of God. Trouble, difficulties and challenges are not necessarily a sign that you are out of the will of God. In fact, these things may indicate that you are doing something right?
>
> (David Cartledge. Australian Evangel. Sept 1997 page 27)

Wow! God was nailing me right from the outset. "Those giants that you are yet to slay Deb will not stop you from fulfilling your purpose as long as you stay focused, stay committed to the journey I am taking you on. Don't miss my signs, my every day confirmations. Keep watch for them so you don't miss one of them."

There would be nothing worse than missing the signposts and finding yourself going around in circles. A total waste of time and energy! Keep your eye on the guide and listen to His voice as He points out each landmark.

MY GOD IS THE CHIEF TOUR GUIDE

Day 2 PROVISION FOR THE DAY

Things don't just fall into your lap do they? Or do they? We were out of food, out of money and needed to feed our kids. Although we had prayed, we made the decision to buy some food on our credit card believing this was our only option at the time.

My family and I were ready to go, credit card in hand when there was a knock at the front door. We opened it to find standing there, good friends of ours from the church. We'd hardly said hello when they blurted out "Hi, we were sitting at home and God told us to come to your place and take you shopping to buy food. He also told us, don't just buy them what they need but whatever they would like and as much of it as they want." My first thought was, God I love these sign posts of Yours!

> Give to others, and you will receive. You will be given much. It will be poured into your hands, more than you can hold. You will be given so much that it will spill into your lap.
> Luke 6:38 (ERV)

We felt like kids in a lolly shop, buying more than we had bought in years. Our kids were asking, "Can we have this, can we have that?" And our amazing friends would say, "Yes, get two of them." We were swimming in God's goodness!

You can be sure that at the very moment you feel like you are going to drown, God will come along, grab you by the hand, lift you up and have you walking on water.

MY GOD IS A GOD WHO IS MORE THAN ENOUGH

_____

Day 3   YOU NEED A HOUSE! I'VE GOT A HOUSE

It was early morning and again there was a knock at the door. This time it was another good friend of ours, Ian. He walked in and straight to the point said, "We have just moved into our new house, but our old house hasn't sold yet. How would you like to go live in it, rent-free until you leave?"

Mmmm, let us think about that, yes, yes, yes please! Wow. That one really knocked our socks off! I couldn't wait to write it in my journal, this 'off the charts' miracle. Thank you, thank you, thank you Jesus. Two weeks later, we'd moved out of our rented home and into Ian's and although this house was on the market for sale, it did not sell until we were on our way to Vietnam. Actually, settlement day for the sale of the house was around the same day we had planned to move out. God orchestrated? I think so.

Sometimes, we can look for provision in the form of money but I think that limits God. On your journey, let God do things His way and you will be surprised, even overwhelmed at His incredible generosity.

> God can do anything, you know—far more than you could ever imagine or guess or request in your wildest dreams! He does it not by pushing us around but by working within us, his Spirit deeply and gently within us.
> Ephesians 3:20-21
> (MSG)

MY GOD WILL DO MORE THAN WE ASK OR IMAGINE

Day 4   WE CAN DO SOMETHING FOR YOU

Our journey also meant we had to raise support. How do you begin asking people for money? We weren't asking, "Hey, can you lend me your car for the day?" or "Can I borrow ten dollars?" Our question was more like, "Hi, we are going to Vietnam for, um, maybe forever. Do you want to support us in that endeavour?" Who in their right mind is going to say yes to that? "Sure, I will support you forever!"

Thank God for friends. Friends are always the best place to start. Paul made that first phone call to a pastor friend of ours. We thought it best we not open with the "Will you support us forever" line. I mean, you have to start off gentle, right? "Hi Dean, how are you doing? We want to share the amazing vision God has put on our hearts. Do you think we could use you as a referee to talk to other pastors?" This was a safe call, we were still learning to stand confident in what God was telling us to do, so for this first contact we thought, let's just ask him to be a character reference for us so we could call other people to ask for money.

> And God is able to make all grace abound toward you, that you, always having all sufficiency in all things, may have an abundance for every good work.
> 2 Corinthians 9:8
> (NKJV)

Knowing God's track record so far on this journey, we should not have been surprised by Dean's response. "Hey, let us support you, and yes, we will give you a character reference, so send us your support pack, we can do something for you. We, as a church will support you."

Let that be noted as day four miracle for us. And can I add right here, that from that day to this, eighteen years later this church is still supporting us.

MY GOD IS A GOD OF ABOVE AND BEYOND

Day 5 CHECK YOUR BANK!

For several years since the downturn of our business, we had learnt to live day by day. Sometimes we weren't sure where the next dollar would come from, but somehow, God would always see us through. Today the electricity bill was due and last time we looked, the last many times we looked, there was no money in the account. I had a part time job at the bank so it was easy for me to check the balance of our account regularly. This was both good and bad because I probably checked it obsessively! I did, however, have to go to the bank to do this because in those days there were no smartphones, or easily accessible Internet, to check online.

I arrived at work and set up for my day, ready to go and just as I always did, checked our account. I felt very nervous because we were not expecting any money, as it was not payday. By faith while holding my breath, I turned the computer on and opened it up to our account. I quickly glanced at the screen and was about to turn away when numbers grabbed my eye. There, in beautiful black and white numbers, was enough money to pay the electricity bill and right then and there God said, "Deb, you panicked about where the money would come from for this bill, but you need to know I am always a God who will be on time. You didn't need the money until the bill was due. Today it is due. Today you have the money. Trust Me."

> Trust in and rely confidently on the Lord with all your heart, and do not rely on your own insight or understanding.
> Proverbs 3:5 (AMP)

While I was learning my lesson on trust, Paul got a phone call from an old friend. "Hey Paul, got some work for you today if you want and I can pay you for it next week." Ok God, I get it!

MY GOD IS A GOD WHO CAN CONFIDENTLY BE RELIED ON

Day 6 OPPORTUNITY TO SPEAK

Although it was only six days into this journey with God, I started to feel like I was living in a whole other dimension with Him during this season. My expectation of just knowing God was going to do something again today, made me feel like every day was Christmas for my family and I, and we were the only ones receiving all the gifts.

All day, and right into the evening, I waited with expectation for God's little gift, but nothing. Not even a sign that there was anything coming, yet I knew in my spirit He would come through for me even at this late hour. God and I had made a deal back on that first day that I wouldn't doubt Him, so even if it got to midnight before God did something or said something, I was sure it would come.

We arrived home just after ten o'clock that evening following a lovely dinner with friends. We put Belinda and Josh to bed and I clicked on the answering machine of our home phone. Yes, that's right, you read correctly, an answering machine. Like I said before, there were no mobile phones then, no instant SMS to check messages from wherever you are in the world. Click, "You have one message." Yes! My heart raced because I knew that this would be it, even before I heard the message, this would be our day six miracle. Hello, this is God speaking. Well actually, "Hi, this is Keith speaking, I have just booked you into a church which is interested in hearing your vision for Vietnam." Ah yes! Another coloured pebble to be cemented into our path with the word Vietnam written on it. Vietnam is your calling and people want to get on board with you.

> My soul, wait silently for God alone, For my expectation is from Him.
> Psalm 62:5 (NKJV)

MY GOD IS IN THE LAST MINUTE

Day 7   WHAT ARE THE KIDS GOING TO SAY?

Any big decision that was made in our home was always discussed as a family. When God called us from our hometown Newcastle to Tasmania, Paul and I didn't just make plans and then tell Belinda and Josh this is what we are going to do. We sat with them, talked about it together and then made the move. They were always great with this, especially when they knew it was something God wanted us to do, but at the age of 11 and 9, it was a little easier for them to be flexible than now at 17 and 15.

Up until this point, we hadn't had the 'let's sit down and chat about our future, kids', talk. For the six days of this journey so far, God had confirmed, provided and spoken. Now we were trusting that God had also prepared our kids. Not that they were unaware of what was happening, but they weren't up on the latest news of us wanting to put a stake in Vietnamese soil with a flag waving from it saying, "Here lies our future."

What Belinda and Josh thought on the matter was important to us and if they were against the whole idea, we would have to rethink our strategy.

That night we sat down with them and talked about what we believed God was saying to us. We already knew Belinda's heart for the street kids in Vietnam so were sure she would be excited about the idea. Our main concern was Josh. Josh had made great friends in Tasmania, he felt at home and was quite settled. He was also at a vulnerable age, 16, so in my mind I was thinking this is going to be a huge deal for him. He may want not want to go. What then?

> Can two people walk together without agreeing on the direction?
> Amos 3:3 (NLT)

Belinda was all smiles, no response was necessary from her, in fact I could almost see her mentally packing her bag to go but what was Josh to think of it all? "Mum and Dad, I am happy to do what God wants us to do, I'll go." And as easy as that, it was decided. In the natural it could have gone either way and that would have been understandable because choosing to say YES to God meant Josh was leaving everything he loved and that was familiar to him. This is not something that would come easy to a mid-teen male. Without a doubt God had gone before us and been working in Josh's heart to prepare him and assure him everything would be all right.

Day 7 was a great day!

MY GOD IS A GOD WHO DESIRES TO UNITE EACH MEMBER TOGETHER

Day 8 DO YOU WANT TO MAKE SOME MONEY?

There was no knock at the door this time but the phone did ring. Before we answered it my heart was jumping inside me. I just knew there was a God something on the other end of that line, another gift from God to unwrap. What would it be? It was a friend of Paul's offering him three days work to earn seventy dollars per day. Now we are talking 1997, so seventy dollars per day was good money. In today's terms it would be the equivalent of around $250 per day, but the job was heavy labouring work and Paul had not done this type of work for a long time. He was a 'collar and tie' businessman.

Remembering James 2:22, needing to have faith like everything depends on God while working (actions) like everything depends on you, we could not expect to sit back and pick and choose what we considered acceptable, and then cry out to God for help. He would always answer back saying, "Have you read James 2:22 lately? That's how I work."

Not everything that God gave us would come easy. Some packages were always going to be prettier than others, but in whatever form it came we needed to take it with a heart of gratitude, a sacrifice of thankfulness.

> 'I have no complaint about your sacrifices, burnt offerings you constantly offer, but you see, I own everything. It is your sacrifice of thankfulness I am looking for.'
> Psalms 50: 8-12 (NLT)

A sacrifice of thankfulness is not a flippant, "Oh thanks, God, for what you have done today." Rather it is purposefully thanking Him from deep within our heart. This pleases the heart of God more than any other sacrifice. Staying grateful, giving a sacrifice of thankfulness is key to keeping the flow of God working in our life.

Paul thankfully accepted this work from his friend and then praised God for what He had provided on this, our day eight.

MY GOD IS A GOD WHO DESIRES OUR SACRIFICE OF THANKFULNESS

Day 9   MANNA FOR THE DAY

I love how God was keeping us grounded so we didn't run away with our imagination of what should happen each day. After yesterday's big injection of finance, it was easy to start thinking, "I wonder how much God is going to give us today? What big thing has He got planned for us next?"

With great expectation, we checked our bank account as we did every day and believed to see big dollars sitting there. Sure enough there were dollars, but not four thousand or even four hundred. There was just forty dollars, but we were grateful because this was God's manna and manna sent from God is always enough. We then noticed written underneath that amount the words, "Designated for Vietnam." We had thanked God for the money, but for what was written underneath was yet another signpost pointing in the direction of Vietnam and that was music to our ears. This was it! This was our God moment for the today.

> Ask the LORD your God for a sign, whether in the deepest depths or in the highest heights.
> Isaiah 7:11 (NIV)
> Our job is to look for the signs.

This journey was not only teaching us lessons of greater trust and faith in God, but also to look for the little things which are really hidden big things.

MY GOD IS A GOD WHO IS SHOUTING OUT LOUD IF YOU ARE LISTENING

Day 10   GOD PREPARES A PLATFORM

In our eagerness to see things happen as quick as we would like, we often try to push doors open that are not ready to be unlocked. When we allow God to do the door opening, however, doors will fling open wide. Trying to do something in our own strength, leaving God out of the picture is like cutting James 2:22 in half. It cannot be just works, it must always be coupled with faith, trusting and leaning in on God. If God is sending us, He will stamp us with His authority, and that God authority will always make a way.

Although we were known in Tasmania, we were not known well enough to stand on a big platform to share our vision. Raising funds for long-term overseas ministry, takes a lot of work and we were doing everything we knew to do, but it was not going to get us to our destiny in the time frame we believed God had given us. It would have been easy to try and push doors that we had no authority to push, but we waited on God to speak to us.

> This is the message from the one who is holy and true, the one who has the key of David. What He opens, no one can close; and what He closes, no one can open.
> Revelation 3:7 (NLT)

Paul often met with Ron Wilson, the ACC Tasmanian State President, to chat about general church business and today was no different, However, on this day as Paul was leaving Ron's office, he said to Paul, "You need to come to our State Pastor's Conference and speak, to share your vision with everyone. As a state, we should support you and as a state, we should send you out."

How's that for an open door, for a big platform? True to God's form, He had already set things in place for us before we asked. He unlocked a door that we thought was not possible to open.

MY GOD IS THE MASTER KEY HOLDER

Day 11   JUDGE AND JURY!

I am so grateful that God is incredibly gracious and patient with us. Today our visa card bill was due and I found myself doing a little freak out dance, crying out to God, asking where the money was going to come from. Now don't judge me too quickly, as I am sure you do the same thing, right? Having a victory one day, then when the next challenge comes your way, allow your eyes to drift back onto your circumstances.

Elijah cheered when he was victorious in defeating Baal only to be found later defeated by fear, anxiety and panic when sent a death message from Jezebel. (1 Kings 18-19 NIV)

The Israelites saw God part the Red Sea to allow them to escape from their captors, miraculously keep their clothing and shoes as good as new throughout the whole forty year journey and provide manna every single day without fail, but the minute there was no water, they complained. What they were really saying was, "God, where are you?"

God knows and understands our weaknesses but He expects our response to come from the truth of His word. "I the Lord your God, do not change." Malachi 3:6 (NIV)

I had panicked because I ran every scenario of where the money could come from through my mind and came up short. How quickly I had forgotten the God who does not change or let me down. One click of a button and I saw once again, the God who was the God of my yesterday be my God of today and as He will be, of my tomorrow. On my computer was a balance of more than enough to pay the visa card and buy food for the week.

> God knows and understands our weaknesses but He expects our response to come from the truth of His word.

My miracle on day eleven came in the form of provision of money and a lesson, and I am glad to learn such a lesson, for I am sure if I hadn't, I would be still walking around in the desert today, never having reached our Promised Land.

These days, eighteen years on, we have to believe God for tens of thousands of dollars regularly for all we do here in Vietnam, and as our ministry continues to grow, so does the need for resource. I can honestly testify to the fact that today I don't worry about where resource is coming from because I have a Malachi 3:6 kind of God.

Don't rely on your feelings, or your limited ability. Rely on the truth of God's Word and His faithfulness.

MY GOD IS A GOD WHO CHANGES NOT

Day 12 WHY SO MANY QUESTIONS?

Fundraising for long-term ministry is a daunting task when you start to analyse how much is needed to fund such a quest. We weren't talking about raising funds for one person, but for our family of four. This was going to be a family deal. Although our hometown was Newcastle, we had been gone from there and the mainland of Australia, for six years. I found myself asking numerous questions that began flooding my mind. Were we going to be able to raise funds from our small network of friends in and around the state of Tasmania? Would we be able to build a strong enough network locally to raise the amount of finance we needed? Do I need to try and get more work? I know we are invited to speak at the State AOG Pastors' Conference, but would they actually listen to us and respond?

I know what you are thinking right now, "My goodness girl, why all these questions? Look at what is happening every day, why are you even

> God affirms us, making us a sure thing in Christ, putting His *YES* within us. By His Spirit He has stamped us with His eternal pledge - a sure beginning of what He is destined to complete.
> 2 Cor 1:21-22 (MSG).
> (emphasis mine)

pondering such things?" Well to answer your question, you need to hear the good, the bad and the ugly so you understand clearly that I am just an ordinary person like you, not perfect, but I walk with an extraordinary God and when an ordinary life gets put into the hands of an extraordinary God, the astonishing, beyond usual takes place and you no longer are classed as ordinary.

It was right in the middle of my day of endless questions, when the phone rang and the ACC State President was on the line. "I wanted to ring you today to let you know that as a church we are going to support you and I want to say to you again that as a state we should rally behind you and corporately send you out, and even if no one else does, I will personally support you." It was like God had answered all those questions in one, to confirm and affirm us. Every morsel that God was giving us was like a big piece of cake and I was grabbing it with both hands.

MY GOD IS A GOD WHO AFFIRMS US

Day 13   BE ENCOURAGED

For a sportsperson there is nothing more encouraging than being cheered from the grandstand by all their fans, hearing shouts of praise echo across the crowds, knowing it's just for them. It causes the player to stand tall and smile from ear to ear, because they know that shout means, "We love you, we believe in you and we are barracking for you." This is the drive that keeps players going and to pushing through to the end, believing they can win.

I like to think of encouragement as an expression of approval and support. It doesn't matter how you feel when you get up in the morning, an encouraging word from someone, or a compliment, can change your whole day. It's like medicine for the soul. Mark Twain once said, "I could live on a good compliment for two months."

The couple whom we were going to assist in the ministry in Vietnam were deported before we even arrived on the ground and that's a whole other story, but this couple came to our church not long after their deportation to share about the ministry and to endorse us. They wanted to encourage us and to inspire our people to get behind us. For this couple to come and in essence say, they were our fans, was not a small thing. Having a long term vision of ministry only to have it cut off suddenly, the last thing you would feel like doing is encouraging and cheering on another couple who were going to be stepping into the shoes you thought belonged to you. That encouragement came from deep within their heart with such a genuine spirit, it blessed us and humbled us beyond measure.

> Since we have such a huge crowd of men of faith watching us from the grandstands, let us strip off anything that slows us down or holds us back.
> Hebrews 12:1 (TLB)

This same day, after receiving such incredible endorsement, we received phone call after phone call from people we hadn't heard from for a long time; friends, pastors, leaders, seemingly out of the blue, ringing us just to encourage us, to cheer us on, to say, we are behind you, we are your fans. You may say, "How is this a miracle day?" I say, "How is it not?" When you are cheered by people like the couple whose shoes you are to fill and by long-time friends who just happened to ring on the same day, you have to know that the cheering was sent from the grandstand of heaven.

Day thirteen, we were encouraged!

MY GOD IS A GOD WHO CHEERS US ON

Day 14   I'VE GOT IT COVERED

It was 9.00 am when the phone rang. Our good friend Brett was on the line already thinking about the logistics of us needing to move into our rent free home on the same weekend as the Pastor's State Conference that was to take place the following week. We had been praying about how we could possibly juggle both moving and being at this significant event at the same time. Both were a big deal. On one hand we were being given the incredible blessing of a home to live in that we didn't have to pay a cent for and on the other a major opportunity to speak to a large gathering, but how were we going to do both?

> Before they call I will answer; while they are still speaking I will hear.
> Isaiah 65:24 (NIV)

"Hey guys, just ringing to let you know that I've been talking to some of our friends and we've organised to move you to your new place while you're at State Conference." Is God amazing or what? There was not one day where God did not show up!

You can be assured that God is not just our majestic Lord, Saviour, healer and deliverer, but He is also an incredible administrator. While you are trying to figure out all the logistics of how things are going to come together, God has already got it covered.

MY GOD IS A GOD WHO ANSWERS BEFORE WE CALL

Day 15   ANOINTED FOR THE TASK

When a soldier is all packed and ready to go to battle, he doesn't just take general supplies, he must also carry reserves. Reserves are what sustain the troops when they have depleted their everyday supplies. We too, must always keep a reserve. If you don't have a reserve, before you know it, your everyday supplies are depleted and you are running on empty, and empty will not get you far. When you are empty, you look for others to sustain you but that is not going to satisfy your soul or your needs at that time. You have to have your own reserve, because it is that reserve which gives you peace, strength and ability, to go another day.

> Now it is God who makes both us and you stand firm in Christ. He anointed us, set His seal of ownership on us, and put His Spirit in our hearts as a deposit, guaranteeing what is to come.
> 2 Corinthians 1:21-22(NIV)

Today God gave us that reserve. A huge deposit of Himself! At church today, as we had hands laid on us to release us as a family into all God had for our future, He saturated us with Himself. We literally felt saturated in God's presence, soaked in His anointing. I knew God was putting a deposit of Himself into us that would sustain us for what lay ahead.

Just because we are called, and living right in the centre of God's will and purposes for our lives, doesn't mean it will be all smooth sailing. There will come times when we need that extra reserve that God has placed in us that will not only sustain us throughout challenging seasons, but also keep us moving forward. Without these deep deposits of God, we know we could not have lasted the distance.

MY GOD IS A GOD WHO GIVES US RESERVES

Day 16 FORTY DOLLARS

It was compulsory for us to attend a nine-week pre-field missions training course before we could head to Vietnam. This was held on the mainland. To get to the mainland we had to catch a boat. To catch the boat, we had to book it and to book it we had to pay a deposit. To pay a deposit, it actually helps to have the money in order to pay.

At this point we hadn't asked how much deposit was needed for a family of four plus our car, because we assumed it would be at least one hundred dollars or more. Living day by day, we didn't have that amount to allocate for this purpose, but time was running out and we really had to book. We knew we couldn't put it off any longer.

We had an appointment with a prospective supporter in the north of the state that day and we were travelling with the couple whom we were originally going to be working with in Vietnam. Before we left, this couple put forty dollars in our hands. We said thank you and thought, "Oh wow, that's nice. Forty dollars." Although we

> Indeed, the very hairs of your head are all numbered. Do not fear; you are more valuable than many sparrows.
> Luke 12:7 (NIV)

knew this was yet another gift from God, we had no idea of the significance of that exact amount when it was handed to us. It wasn't fifty dollars, or even forty five dollars, it was exactly forty dollars.

Paul finally did get around to ringing the Spirit of Tasmania booking office to find out how much deposit we needed for the boat. I don't recall if it was on this day or not, but the scenario went something like this:

"Good morning, Spirit of Tasmania." "Hi, I am just (hesitantly) ringing to find out how much deposit we would need to pay for a family of four with a car one way on the boat?" "For a family of four, with a car, the minimum deposit is forty dollars." Oh my goodness…forty dollars… are you kidding me? Wow! Forty dollars, of course it is!

Do I have to say any more?

> **MY GOD IS THE GOD OF THE FORTY DOLLARS, THE HUNDRED, THE THOUSAND, THE EXACT AMOUNT YOU NEED!**

Day 17
A FAMILY JOURNEY

We were being blessed by so many people in hundreds of different ways, encouraged by long time friends and new ones, finance was flowing big and small, through channels totally unexpected, and God's anointing was filling us up for the road ahead, but this journey did not just involve Paul and myself. This journey also included our two children Belinda who was 17 at the time, and Josh who was 15. As I said before, whenever we made major decisions in life, Paul and I didn't just sit our kids down and say, "This is what we are doing so you need to be ok with it." That was not the way we operated as a family. We always chatted through everything. If our kids were against this whole new season of life for us, we would have had to rework what this future of ours was going to look like.

Belinda had had some struggles throughout our time in Tasmania. Leaving our hometown Newcastle was not an easy move for her, so to take on this even greater move was something that played heavily on her spirit. It wasn't that she didn't want to go. In fact she was very excited about it, knowing she could work with street kids, something that had been in her heart to do since she was a small child herself. However, at seventeen, she wanted to get something from God that was specifically for her, to build her own reserve pack.

She had not had a great deal of contact with friends back in Newcastle over the six years we were living in Tasmania so to receive a phone call out of the blue from an old friend who just felt to contact her and encourage her, blessed Belinda's spirit and it was the very thing that filled her tank, giving her the armour she needed for her own road ahead. Seeing God come through for her today, definitely counted as our day seventeen for me, God speaking loud, saying I have all of you covered.

> Behold, children are a gift of the Lord, the fruit of the womb is a reward. Like arrows in the hand of a warrior, so are the children of one's youth. How blessed is the man whose quiver is full of them
> Psalm 127:3-5 (NASB)

If you are married with children, taking your kids along on your adult journey, which God has you on, that gets you out of your comfortable life to fulfill the call He has for you, can be a major concern. You ask yourself, how will they cope? What will it do to them?

Several years ago I read somewhere about a survey that was taken regarding children who'd succeeded in life. These children had grown up with parents in top vocations such as doctors, lawyers, dentists, accountants, pastors and others including missionaries, and missionary kids were found to be in the top ten percent of those who had succeeded. Yes that's right, you heard me, kids who left their comfortable every day with their parents to do the unusual, beyond normal in a foreign land. I hear you saying very clearly now, "Oh no, no, no, I don't want to be a missionary!" Well, I am not saying you have to be one in the traditional sense, not all are called to go overseas, but all of us are called to missions whether that is in our own backyard or in someone else's.

Whatever God is calling you to do, know this, God is a God of family and He doesn't just have you covered. He has your children covered also. Handle the journey well and they will come out on top.

MY GOD IS THE GOD OF ABRAHAM
AND ALL HIS DESCENDANTS

Day 18 DOWN PAYMENT MADE

> Whoever keeps staring at the wind won't sow; whoever daydreams won't reap.
> Ecclesiastes 11:4 (ISV)

Remember that forty dollars? Well today Paul went in and paid that forty dollars as a deposit for the boat trip to the mainland. Making this down payment today meant we were no longer just planning and talking about our future. We were actually lifting one foot off our old season and putting it onto the new. It was an amazing feeling to be able to tangibly do something that propelled us forward. I was excited and nervous at the same time because this also meant the leap of faith I was trusting God for was now being put into action. The wheels were now in motion. It reminded me of the first time I ventured onto a big roller coaster, I was excited about the adventure, but at the same time questioning, "Do I really want to do this? It's a long way to the top," but with determination in my mind, I got in line and before I knew it, I was at the gate and it was my turn. "I can do this!" Roller coasters and I have not been companions since then, but leaping onto God rides has.

Also today more people contacted us, championing our cause and asking us to send support letters to them. This goes to show that every single day, God was turning up in one way or another to say the path we were on, was indeed the right one.

MY GOD IS THE GOD WHO TAKES US
ON AMAZING JOURNEYS

Day 19   STRIKING A ROCK IF NECESSARY

As you read through this book/journal of mine, it is easy to glide through in a few moments of time, reading my written thoughts followed by the revelations God gave me on the journey and think, that's nice or that's good, with not too much thought. However, when you are the one walking in it, day by day, hour by hour and sometimes minute by minute, it becomes a focused, all engrossing step by step faith walk. I am very conscious of this fact when reading the lives of those in Biblical history. We read their journey and think "wow," but between the journey and the wows there were a lot of day by day, hour by hour and minute by minute faith, pushing through moments for them also.

> He raised his stick in the air and struck the rock two times. At once, water gushed from the rock, and the people and their livestock had water to drink.
> Numbers 20:11 (CEV)

I woke up this morning feeling vulnerable and in need of more specifics from God. I don't know why, it was just there. I am sure the enemy had a lot to do with it, trying to discourage me, but I knew walking this walk of the extraordinary, thoughts like this would come.

We can all have these moments but they seem to come more often when you step out of your comfort zone to do what God is asking you to do. During those times it is easy to condemn yourself for it, and you can have a tendency to want to beat yourself up for thinking this way, calling yourself an unbelieving Israelite. We must not do this, for you see the Israelites chose to stay in their unbelief, but we on the other hand, acknowledge that although we are to expect these thoughts to come, faith must rise above emotion and continue to move us forward with hearts expectant for what God will do next, saying, "God I believe, but help me in my unbelief."

We had just finished music practice at our house and after saying goodbye to everyone, I went to the fridge to get a drink and there in the fridge (Would you believe?) was an envelope. On the front of the envelope was written, "This $50 is to help you get to the conference you are speaking at." Haha, in the fridge! For us it was the fridge, for the Israelites it was in a rock! Moses struck a rock and out came water. There you go, you Israelites, in the most unexpected places, God can provide what you need.

Another unexpected gift that night was from one of the girls in the music team who said she would be responsible for all our newsletters to be sent out. To comprehend how huge this was in 1998, you have to understand that this was the pre-electronic email and websites days. You typed your newsletter (on a computer, at least we had that), stood for hours as you printed hundreds of hardcopies, hand wrote all the envelopes to make it personal, placed a stamp on every one and then sent them out. I am so happy we can now send an email newsletter to countless people in seconds. For you who are just starting out, know how blessed you are with today's modern technology. No need to tap on a rock for this one!

MY GOD IS THE GOD OF THE UNEXPECTED PLACES

Day 20 SET UP

This was a big day for us, starting out on this untraveled road. The opportunity to share our vision with a whole state was nothing short of a miracle to us. To have the ear of pastors local, state and visiting from the mainland and abroad, was a huge blessing, and we were feeling both excited and anxious.

The overseas guest speaker began his first message out of Isaiah 49:8 which spoke of the restoration of a nation. This pastor had no idea of our presence in that meeting, but that word went straight into our spirits like a rushing wind, capturing every fibre of our being. "He is speaking to us." God was saying, "I am calling you to be a restorer of a nation. This is what your journey is about. This is what your day by day preparation is for, so you are equipped for the days ahead." What an enormous injection into our faith, our spirit and our hearts. At the end of his message a guest singer, who had just moved to Australia three weeks prior, stood up and sang a song called, "Who will go where there is darkness." Before he had begun the second verse we were totally undone. Everything we'd been feeling, believing for, trusting in, pushing through to, had been totally encapsulated through the message spoken and the song sung.

At the end of that God-breathed song we were invited up to share our vision. We could not have asked for a better launching platform, a word that spoke of broken nations needing to be restored and a song that beckoned people to go. It seemed that God had set everything up just for us. We poured our hearts out, shared our passion for the nation God desired us to see restored and proclaimed that we were ready to go after which the state president called on the whole state to not only stand behind us but to support us and send us out. There are no words to fully describe this moment except to say, only God!

> The Spirit of the Sovereign Lord is upon me, for the Lord has anointed me to bring good news to the poor. He has sent me to comfort the brokenhearted and to proclaim that captives will be released and prisoners will be freed. He has sent me to tell those who mourn that the time of the Lord's favour has come, and with it, the day of God's anger against their enemies. To all who mourn in Israel, he will give a crown of beauty for ashes, a joyous blessing instead of mourning, festive praise instead of despair. In their righteousness, they will be like great oaks that the Lord has planted for his own glory.
> Isaiah 61:1-3 (NLT)

What was meant to be an ACC State Leaders Conference, became very much a missions conference, beating to the drum of God's heartbeat, His mission field.

MY GOD IS THE GOD OF DEFINING MOMENTS FOR HIS OWN GLORY

Day 21   THOSE LITTLE DISTRACTIONS

Distractions. Those other things that divert our attention from the main thing.

When Jesus called people to follow Him in Luke 9:57-62 their response was, "I can't, I have this to do or that to do." These individuals were totally distracted by the lesser things they needed to do in life, and totally missed out on the God opportunity of a lifetime. It was not that their other duties were unimportant, nor were they to be neglected, but they allowed the issues of life to take the place of God's call on their life. If we are not careful, we can justify things that put urgent demands on us as the reason we can't fulfill our destiny.

What do we keep, what do we sell, what do we give away? Who is going to take care of the belongings we want to keep while we are gone, for however long that is? Who is willing to take our cat? Do we keep the car for visits or do we sell the car? How can we get everything done before we leave this state?

> Instead, be concerned above everything else with the Kingdom of God and with what he requires of you, and he will provide you with all these other things.
> Matt 6:33 (GNT)

I am glad our response to God wasn't, "We can't." We were

very much in boots and all. However, these things were definitely becoming a big distraction and we knew it. In saying YES to God, we had to make a decision to put all requests out there to friends, trust God to have a solution for each one and keep our eyes on following Jesus. With this set in our spirit, our focus was turned back to the important, and because we did this, today many of our friends rallied around us to take care of these little things we had been concerned about for way too long.

If only those who Jesus called to follow Him had just trusted Him to take care of their other obligations and followed the call on their life, they would have discovered a God who is just as concerned about their duties as they were. I know it is a well used phrase, but when you are taking care of God's business, He will take care of yours, and He did this for us today.

For us, it was another day in miracle journey paradise.

MY GOD IS THE GOD WHO TAKES CARE OF LITTLE THINGS

Day 22   ANOTHER STEP CLOSER

Hebrews 11:1 (MSG) says, "Faith is the firm foundation under everything that makes life worth living." How true this is, and we were seeing just how worthwhile this faith trip was as we moved into our rent free, electricity free, phone free house, the house that was one of the first miracles given to us as we began this two hundred day journey.

This precious gift was going to take a huge financial burden off our shoulders, which also meant money that we usually had to find for these large expenses could now be allocated toward getting to our destination.

Physically moving from what had been our permanent home to this temporary place meant we were now in a state of transition. There were adjustments to be made as we felt our stake being levered out of the Tasmanian soil and sitting on no-man's land. However, overall, we were excited. For us this transition time was relatively short, but transition for some, can seem long and drawn out, often leaving them wondering if they will ever get to the other side. There are two points I want to make about transitions. Firstly, is that you have to go with them. You cannot have your nails embedded into what was or you won't birth what will be. Secondly, transitions are just that. They are not destinations, so you don't have to worry about it being an endless period of time unless you don't follow the rule of point number one.

> For I am about to do something new! See, I have already begun! Do you not see it? I will make a pathway through the wilderness. I will create rivers in the dry wasteland
> Isaiah 43:19 (NLT)

"The secret to change is to focus all your energy, not on fighting the old, but on building the new."
- SOCRATES

MY GOD IS THE GOD WHO WALKS WITH US IN THE VALLEY OF TRANSITIONS

Day 23
STAY HUMBLE, YOU MIGHT LEARN SOMETHING!

I think one of the most encouraging things to experience when you are on your own journey through life, is to listen to stories of other people's journeys, to glean from their experiences and take on board any wise advice they may have. Staying teachable and humble spirited will actually launch us further in our own walk if we take the time to do this. I learnt this lesson very early on when I was speaking at a women's conference in the north of the state of Tasmania. I was privileged to share that stage with a well-known, worldwide speaker. After one of the meetings we sat down together and she began asking me lots of questions about family and how I kept our family healthy while doing ministry. I couldn't believe a seasoned speaker who had a large ministry of her own, was asking me these questions. Although I did answer her questions, I had to ask her, why would she, who is so advanced in ministry, be asking me these things? She told me something I will never forget. She said, "Wherever I go and whoever I meet, I try to learn something from people I engage with that will help me grow. I always want to remain a learner and I believe we can all learn from each other."

> And he said to them, "Pay attention to what you hear: with the measure you use, it will be measured to you, and still more will be added to you.
> Mark 4:24 (ESV)

I have to admit, had I not learnt this lesson of gleaning from others who had been on journey's of their own, I could have missed out on valuable insight due to (I am ashamed to say) judgmental thinking, picking and choosing who I thought would be good to learn from and who would not. This night we were going to a meeting to hear from a man who had, in the past, lived and served overseas for a period of time. We knew this person well in his role as a Bible school lecturer and although he was a lovely man, he spoke quite monotone. Knowing this about him it would have been easy for me to form the opinion that he would be boring and I probably wouldn't get anything out of it either. I was definitely saved by the wisdom of that well-known pastor during the women's conference I had attended. I learnt to lean in wherever I went, and this night I gained a wealth of knowledge from the experience and lessons this man shared from his time on foreign soil. It was gold for us.

God had dropped a fabulous nugget of wisdom into my lap today, a reminder that there was gold in many places and to keep my ears, my eyes and my hands open to receive them because they would serve me and my family well when the need arose.

MY GOD IS THE GOD WHO GIVES US AN EAR TO HEAR

Day 24
WHERE DID YOU SAY WE WERE GOING ,GOD?

In 1997, Vietnam was definitely not on the tourist map. When mentioning Vietnam to anyone at that time, most responses were, "Oh isn't that where there was a war?" We even had some say, "Where's that?" To bump into people who knew about Vietnam, let alone had been there, was unusual. I got chatting with a new girl who had just started working at the bank and she told me that she had just come back from holidays before starting her job. I asked her where she had gone for her vacation and the conversation went something like this; "So where did you go for your holidays?" "I've just come back from Vietnam." "Really! Vietnam, really? No one goes to Vietnam for a holiday. Why Vietnam?" (At that time it was not a popular holiday destination). She started to tell me how amazing it was and that it is somewhere people should visit. I could hardly contain myself. Anyone who knows me, knows I am quite animated. I tried to stay calm but eventually I just couldn't help myself and preceded to tell her at one hundred miles an hour about our call to Vietnam. I'm not sure if she wanted to hear it or not, but she seemed excited for us. I was on a high all day just hearing about her adventures in the land we were called to. I couldn't believe someone had gone there for a holiday.

> For God does speak now one way, now another though no one perceives it.
> Job 33:14 (NIV)
> Keep listening!!

When I got home from work I couldn't wait to tell Paul about meeting this new girl who had actually gone to Vietnam on a holiday. As we are chatting, I flicked on the television and a show called Get Away was just starting. This show highlights great holiday destinations of the world and tonight, there in our living room, the commentator broadcast to us that they were showcasing a new destination, Vietnam. "What! Are you kidding me?" The odds of coming in contact with our calling twice in one day, was uncanny. "So God, would it be Vietnam You are calling us to?"

Tuesday 14th October 1997 was a memorable day. We found money under our front door mat and approval was given to me for long term leave from my job (although I didn't expect to be back) and God was saying loud and clear Vietnam, Vietnam, Vietnam!

> **MY GOD IS A GOD WHO SPEAKS TO US THROUGH MANY AVENUES.
> ONCE HE USED A DONKEY,
> SO DON'T LIMIT HOW HE SPEAKS TO YOU**

Day 25 PUTTING GOD FIRST

Believing for finance and provision daily can be a worrying thing if your trust is in you and not God. Having two teenage children in high school and needing to feed, clothe and buy endless school supplies for them did not come cheap. Then there were those nasty business bills that were too big to jump over, and on top of this Paul had to go to Melbourne for meetings with our mission agency and there were no such things as cheap flight deals in those days. I was working in the bank, but it was only a part time position so in the natural, my wage never covered all these things.

Financial hardship is very real and can consume you. It is very easy to look at every dollar that comes in and immediately think, how can I make this do the impossible? The temptation to put the little you have into the pressing needs can cause you to justify not giving to God.

When two hundred and sixty dollars came into Paul's hand today we felt that same pressure. We had to decide, do we pay for the airfare to get Paul to Melbourne, which was a must, or do we give first fruits to God and believe He will come up with the money for this need that was due?

> In everything you do, put God first, and he will direct you and crown your efforts with success.
> Proverbs 3:6 (TLB)

When you feel caught between a rock and a hard place, you are certainly tested on whether you indeed believe God at His word and that He will come up with the goods for you. Of course it was a no brainer to give God what was rightfully His first even though the alternative may have crossed our mind.

Having the thought, and acting on that thought, are two completely different things. We will doubt daily, even hourly, but the choice we make following those thoughts, makes all the difference in God's world. Remember, He acts on our faith to believe.

After giving to God what was rightfully His, we had enough left to pay the other small bills due, but absolutely no money at all for the airfare. Paul told me he was going to ring the airline to see if we had any frequent flyer points. I cannot remember my exact response, but it definitely came with some sarcasm. I had calculated the flight points and we didn't even have enough to get to the next town let alone to another state. "Yes, let's just do that, I am sure that we will have plenty." As usual my faith filled husband's response was, "God will provide!" So he pushed on that door and when he got off the phone he said, "Well I am on my way to Melbourne, free." I was floored once again. God showed Himself true in response to faith and once again, God got me!

Lesson learnt. Let go and let God work outside the box. We can try and figure it all out and then God does something that says, "I am God, you're not."

MY GOD IS A GOD WHO WORKS OUTSIDE THE BOX

Day 26
MELBOURNE BOUND BUT NOWHERE TO STAY

As I said before, at this stage, our sphere of influence was Newcastle and Tasmania. We knew no one in Melbourne. Paul was now on his way there for free, but he had nowhere to lay his head. We talked a lot about cheap hotels, but realistically we couldn't even do that. Paul said, "I'm going to ring the mission office to see if they can help."

This was to be the very first interview regarding our call to Vietnam by our mission agency so we knew they would be checking us out thoroughly. Who are these Hiltons anyway? Are they the right people to go? Are they prepared? Do they have everything in order? We knew these and other questions would be on the minds of those doing the interview so the thought of ringing them to ask for a bed was a bit of a bold move. Our answers to their questions would be sure, yes, we are called, yes we are getting things in order, yes we are prepared as much as we can be, but we don't have a bed or means for a bed to sleep on when Paul gets to see you in Melbourne.

I felt very hesitant about Paul asking for such a favour, but in reality I should have known better because, after all, this was a mission, not a business. Their response was without question. "Let's see what we can do for you," and within hours they had rung Paul back with a place for him to stay. Amazing. Free airfare and now free board. The hosts may I say, looked after Paul like a king. They couldn't do enough for him, blessing him in every way possible. God had not only made a way but He'd laid out the red carpet for Paul, making him feel special. For me, it was a great reminder that we are indeed the King's kids and God always takes care of His own.

> The Lord is my Shepherd, I shall not want and He makes me to lie down in green pastures
> Psalm 23: 1-2 (NKJV)

Get out of your comfort boat people, and see God take care of everything. God's daily provision is indescribable.

**MY GOD IS A GOD WHO MAKES US
LAY DOWN IN GREEN PASTURES**

Day 27 THE WORD MOTIVATES AND FEED US

Zig Ziglar, a world known motivational speaker once said at a meeting I attended,

> "It takes a good seventeen times to believe and act on something you have been told. At first you hear it, and it is simply information that passes between your two ears. Then the next few times you hear it, it becomes a familiar message that sounds like a good idea. After that, your ears prick up and you listen more intently, because it is starting to make sense to you. You even believe this is good for someone else. Eventually, you begin to take notice of what is being said as something that you need for yourself, but it isn't until around the seventeenth time that you consciously pick it up and put it into practice."

I am hoping by now James 2:22 is getting under your skin to the point that you are grabbing it with both hands and running with it. Faith without works is dead. Faith and works go hand in hand. If you separate body and spirit, you have a corpse. If you separate faith and works, you are left with a carcass.

I cannot stress enough that this is the secret in seeing God move. When He looks down and sees us doing and serving with a heart totally sold out for Him, He says, "This is the kind of person I can use and I will open doors for them, because they have wheels under their feet." You can have all the heart for God you want, but if you are still sitting waiting for God to do something first, you have it the wrong way around. He only works with moving vehicles.

God continually points me back to this verse so I never forget that it is all about moving and believing. Today my gift from Him was the timely reminder of how powerful this word truly is. I had heard it enough times for it to be in my action plan to stay motivated, to continue moving forward and not looking back, but reading it again today, allowing it to soak into my spirit once again, helped me throw down the waves of doubt that so often washed over me.

> Do you see that faith was working together with his works, and by works faith was made perfect?
> James 2:22 (NKJV)

The extraordinary in us is merely being willing to move, being willing to just say YES to God. We're not over the top, extraordinary, more highly favoured people due to saintliness, but purely because we stay moving vehicles in the hands of God. Remaining in this place of momentum is what has allowed us to build a ministry that is seeing countless lives transformed by the power of God, not just in Vietnam but Asia wide and beyond. The formula is not complicated. Stand up, move one step at a time, love God, serve Him where you are right now, giving Him the glory for it and watch what He will do with your life.

MY GOD IS A GOD WHO WORKS WITH MOVING VEHICLES

Day 28   IS THAT FOR SALE?

We were settling into our temporary home as best we could, knowing this was our in-between place, that place of leaving the secure, to launch into the unsecure, and it felt quite surreal. At this point there were still plenty of opportunities for us to say, "Let's stop right here," and we could have been forgiven for it, but our motivation to keep going, besides wanting to do God's will, was seeing Him show up every day.

We were cleaning up the garage of our short-term residence, sorting through all of our belongings that had been put in there by our helpful friends who moved us. As we were doing this, people started coming in, seemingly from nowhere and right into our garage. I was thinking, "Who are these people, our welcoming committee?" One of these unexpected visitors spoke up and said, "So, which of these items are for sale?" We had planned on having a garage sale once we had sorted through what we would keep, throw away, give away, take with us, and ultimately sell, but we had just moved in and were not remotely ready for that. However, without missing a beat, we started naming items that were for sale and began what became an impromptu garage sale and sold several major items. It was amazing. I believe God was saying to us right then and there, "You have lots to organise, let me bring them to you without all the fuss and bother."

> Two of every kind of bird, of every kind of animal and of every kind of creature that moves along the ground will come to you to be kept alive. Genesis 6:20 (NIV)
> Two of every kind of bird, of every kind of animal and of every kind of creature that moves along the ground will come to you to be kept alive. Genesis 6:20 (NIV)

When Noah was to gather all the animals into the ark, you will notice in Genesis 6:19-20 that he didn't go out and do the entire gathering. In verse 20, it states very clearly, "Pairs of every kind of bird, and every kind of animal, and every kind of small animal that scurries along the ground, will come to you to be kept alive." God brought them to Noah.

It was the best unprepared garage sale we had ever run. We did go on to have other garage sales before we left that place, but this day was a great lesson in knowing God loves to give us a hand up.

Our Vietnam fund was now starting to grow and we were half way to paying our mission training fees!

**MY GOD IS MY LIGHTHOUSE.
HE DREW LOTS OF PEOPLE TO US TODAY**

Day 29 PROPHESY

It's Sunday morning, which for us meant another opportunity to share our vision at yet another church. Paul preached first and then together, we shared our hearts for the nation of Vietnam. No sooner had we finished our presentation, and the pastor was on his feet saying, "God has given me a word for you both." Getting a prophesy during this time, any word from God was like medicine to us. Yes please, bring it on! We'll take the whole bottle thanks.

Prophesy should confirm what you already sense in your spirit or at least resonate in some way that it is a God word. Once you get given this word however, what should you do with it? I can tell you what you shouldn't do with it, and that's try to make it happen in your own strength.

If it is a word that confirms what you are already doing, or about to launch into, there may be things you need to put into place in readiness for that word to be birthed. If however, it is a word that resonates with you, but not in your mind's eye at this time, you can safely put in on a shelf, knowing that God will open that box for you when it is the right time. It may be tomorrow, next month, next year or sometime down the track, but it will become a reality for you once God knows you are ready for it and it is the right season.

> Many are the plans in the mind of a man, but it is the purpose of the Lord that will stand.
> Proverbs 19:21 (ESV)

The prophesy we received on this day was incredible. Too long to put it all down here, but the short version was that Paul was to receive a new anointing, wisdom to speak to leaders, to Government in places where doors had been shut before, that he would not be afraid to speak into their lives and it would come with wisdom and knowledge speaking right into their lives, even personal things, and he would say them without fear. It would be like an arrow hitting the target and also God would open doors in places others have struggled to get in. For me, I would be just as my name says, that I would rise up as a Deborah, gathering women from all over and they would draw from me like a mother of Israel.

Our first response was, "Wow this is incredible," but then there was the thought, "How can this be? We are going to Vietnam to be administrators for another couple, to be their hands lifted up, behind the scenes servants, not the front people." The word did sound amazing though. We loved it. It did resonate in us. We totally accepted it, but thought this one seems to be one for the shelf at this point.

At the time of receiving this word, we had no idea what was to unfold when we landed in Vietnam. The plan was that we would assist another couple intending to return to the country not long after we arrived. However, they were not allowed to re-enter that nation again. This meant we would became assistants to ourselves and leadership was to be thrust into our hands.

**MY GOD IS A GOD WHO KNOWS
THE BEGINNING FROM THE END**

Day 30
ANOTHER DAY ANOTHER INJECTION OF A DOLLAR

See what great love the Father has lavished on us, that we should be called children of God! And that is what we are! 1 John 3:1 (NIV)

The further along in this journey I go, the more I am seeing the Father heart of God. As wonderful as this is though, I don't think I will fully grasp just how deep, how wide, how high and vast His love truly reaches. None of us will know the full extent of this love until we see Him face-to-face. We just have to believe and be assured that God truly is love.

> How great is the goodness you have stored up for those who fear you. You lavish it on those who come to you for protection, blessing them before the watching world.
> Psalm 31:19 (NLT)

We had thought of doing a fundraiser for our ministry, but really didn't know if it was the right thing to do. Should we really be asking others to raise funds for us? Maybe we could do something small that wouldn't be so intrusive on the church. After all, the new pastor was now on the scene and he was not thrilled that we were leaving. It wasn't because he didn't like us or didn't believe that God was calling us, he was just hoping we would stay around. We were completely surprised when he called us today to let us know that the church intended to organise a fundraiser for us. Not some small bake off event but a full blown, sit down dinner, live music, invite to one and all across the city, affair. Pastor Keith had put his own desires aside to lavish upon us this incredible blessing.

What Keith was planning for us was so much bigger than we had anticipated doing for ourselves. This in essence is what God is telling us in 1 John 3:1. "You think I love you this much when in fact I love you so much that I desire to spoil you extravagantly."

Every day, more funds, and promises of funds began to come in. It wasn't just occasionally now, but more often than not. A Bible college emailed to say it would taking up a love offering for us and we continued to have non-stop people coming to our door to buy more items from our 'garage sale.' A garage sale that just kept on going.

MY GOD IS A GOD WHO LAVISHES UPON US

Day 31 LOCATION, LOCATION, LOCATION

I had to laugh when I reread my journal notes for this day. Would you believe, more people turned up at our door wanting to buy items from our 'garage sale.' Several groups of people in fact! I don't know what your experience is of garage sales, but it's usually hard work. First, there's the printing of flyers after which you run around your whole area posting them on every pole you can find only to discover you have to jockey for position with all those other people who have their own signage up to beckon people to come to their garage sale. Then you wait from dawn until dusk hoping people will stop and come in. You even have your kids waving to every passing car to please stop and come and look at your prized possessions because they will be glad they did, and by the end of the day you are exhausted because you have bargained with those buyers to please just pay a little more. You count up your sales money and wonder, was that whole exercise worth it. For us though, we had people flocking to our door, not just on the allotted garage sale day, but also for many days and weeks after, day and night. This was not normal.

> God can pour on the blessings in astonishing ways so that you're ready for anything and everything, more than just ready to do what needs to be done.
> 1 Corinthians 9:8 (MSG)

I know God positioned us in this home for such a time as this for many reasons, and to sell our wares was one of them. We did try and have a garage sale in the home we were renting before moving into this house, but our experience was just like everyone else's, an uphill battle.

You have to know God was supernaturally drawing people to our location. Every day is an amazing adventure with God.

> **MY GOD IS A GOD WHO POSITIONS US FOR THE UNUSUAL TO TAKE PLACE!**

Day 32   IN TIMES OF STRUGGLES AND TRUST

When we arrived in Tasmania, we bought a business that we believed would support us while serving in ministry. However, this business, although we had it checked by our lawyers, was not all it appeared to be on paper. That is a whole other story I won't go into, but the fallout from buying this so-called successful enterprise, meant we were left on the brink of bankruptcy as we tried to turn it around and do the right thing by our clients. In the natural, this mountain of debt that continued to rise, was way too high to jump over, and it was a constant struggle to keep motivated to believe for a better day. For us, not every day was an 'up' day. We often had to push through feelings of discouragement when we felt God was far from us.

Despite our circumstances, as every dollar came into our hands we stayed committed to giving God the first fruits no matter what, then we would pay whatever bills we could.

Throughout our six year 'Bible school of life' in Tasmania, regardless of our financial struggles due to this failing business, God always kept food on our table, our children in school, house rent paid for (while living in rental properties), and miraculously funded mission trips to Vietnam. From natural resources, it was not the business that provided for us, but my part time salary from the bank. Then God would supernaturally touch the little we had and multiply, grow or stretch it to do what it needed to do for us in every situation.

Today was a day like every other day in that we needed to believe for finance to pay off more pressing bills that screamed at our business door. Our natural response was to stress out. To be honest, there was often a tinge of doubt and unbelief in us as each situation arose; however, we would manage to put aside those feelings and get down to prayer, asking God to come through somehow and tell us what we needed to do in that circumstance.

Later that day the Bond Board rang us to give us their answer on whether we were to receive our bond money back, or not. This is the organisation that holds a bond amount you pay to them when making a contract with owners of a home you wish to rent. If you are good tenants, you will get your bond money back at the end of your lease. It is not always a guarantee that you will get the full amount returned to you as they go through the property with a fine-toothed comb. Even if you have been a first class tenant, careful with everything in the house, they will often find something you need to pay for.

When Paul told me it was the Bond Board on the phone I was nervous but that feeling was soon laid to rest when he told me the board had agreed to give us a full refund. "Your total bond has been released from your rental property today. You can come and pick it up at your convenience."

> This High Priest of ours understands our weaknesses, for He faced all of the same testings we do, yet He did not sin.
> Hebrews 4:15 (NTL)

Pick it up at your convenience!
Our convenience was today, right now in fact.
In our humanity, we will struggle. The struggle will test our faith, but amidst this struggle we have to believe God is still Jehovah Jireh.

MY GOD IS A GOD IN THE STRUGGLE

Day 33 THE WORD MAKES EVERYTHING RIGHT

Rejoice in the Lord always. I will say it again. Rejoice in the Lord always. "Rejoice! Let your gentleness be evident to all. The Lord is near. Do not be anxious about anything, but in every situation, by prayer and petition, with thanksgiving, present your requests to God. And the peace of God, which transcends all understanding, will guard your hearts and your minds in Christ Jesus." Philippians 4:4-7 (NIV)

Peace was exactly what I needed today as I became overwhelmed by everything that still needed to be done before leaving. The enemy loves to get to us before we begin our day to keep us from being productive and proactive in our call. He was trying it on me today. "Look at all the things you need to do. You're not going to get everything done, why don't you just give up."

> And the peace of God, which transcends all understanding, will guard your hearts and your minds in Christ Jesus.
> Philippians 4:7 (NIV)

I am so glad God's Word was becoming more and more part of my daily confession as I read intently to find medicine for my soul and the blueprint for my destiny. As the enemy was trying to bring me down, the Word of God lifted me straight back up. It's amazing how worry can be pounding at your door, but a few words from the living word puts everything back in perspective and peace comes. The Word makes everything right.

You cannot put a price on heaven's peace. When you get that kind of peace, nothing shakes you. It's a peace that is completely beyond understanding (Philippians 4:7). When people see us with that kind of peace in the midst of great turmoil, it reveals the greater source from which it comes, God.

MY GOD IS A GOD OF PEACE

Day 34 CAR DETAILS

Before heading to Vietnam, we had to go to Sydney to attend our missions training course. Paul was to go ahead of us and start the training while I remained in Tasmania for Belinda and Josh to finish their school year. We would then join him and I would catch up on this training. Having to go later meant I was to drive from Tasmania to Sydney on my own with our kids. Our Subaru car, although still reliable, was now getting old and I was concerned about its reliability to get us safely to Sydney. I had no mechanical knowledge, which meant if anything other than petrol or oil was needed for the car, I would be stuck!

I both loved and loathed the sound of the postman when he arrived. Was it going to be another bill or could I believe for a God surprise? I had come to expect the unexpected even in the mail during this amazing journey. Today it was a letter from the Subaru dealership. My first thought was, "Oh do we owe them some money." Several months earlier we had had some work done on the car but I was sure we had paid them. Nevertheless, like everything else, we were paying bills off as money came in, so I couldn't be sure this was not a reminder notice. I didn't want to open the letter, but knew I couldn't ignore it either. I had to open it no matter what it said.

"Dear Subaru owner, we would like to offer you a free oil change and safety check on your car. Please make an appointment for your free service!"

If I could have high fived God right then and there, I would have. What a huge weight off my mind and a brilliant day 34. I could now travel this long distance with peace of mind.

> The Lord will keep you from all harm - he will watch over your life.
> Psalm 121:7 (NIV)

And just on a side note, our never ending garage sale was still receiving visitors who told their friends to tell their friends to come on down to buy from us. Our stuff really wasn't that great. You have to know that this was totally a God thing.

MY GOD IS A GOD WHO KEEPS US SAFE

Day 35 - 36 LITTLE FLASK, BIG JARS

> Elisha asked. "Tell me, what do you have in the house?" "Nothing at all, except a flask of olive oil," she replied. And Elisha said, "Borrow as many empty jars as you can from your friends and neighbors. Then go into your house with your sons and shut the door behind you. Pour olive oil from your flask into the jars, setting each one aside when it is filled." So she did as she was told. Her sons kept bringing jars to her, and she filled one after another. Soon every container was full to the brim!
>
> "Bring me another jar," she said to one of her sons. "There aren't any more!" he told her. And then the olive oil stopped flowing. When she told the man of God what had happened, he said to her, "Now sell the olive oil and pay your debts, and you and your sons can live on what is left over." 2 Kings 4:3 (NIV)

This is a perfect example of how God can use our little and to do much. The widow received all she needed, paid her debts and lived on what was left over.

This is exactly what was happening with us every day. The oil we had was the gear in our garage. I am not kidding when I say to you, people were coming almost daily to our house to buy things from our garage store. As God sent people to buy, we would pour that oil into jars that needed filling and found we still had enough left over to live on. In the natural it didn't add up, it was a miracle.

I believe that when Jesus told the disciples to feed the five thousand, that little boy who gave his five loaves and two fish was probably not the first person the disciples approached, but he was the first one to release his food into God's hand. I have to wonder just how many people were asked to share their food before they got to this little boy.

> Now He who supplies seed to the sower and bread for food will also supply and increase your store of seed and will enlarge the harvest of your righteousness.
> 2 Corinthians 9:10 (NIV)

How many had said, "No" out of fear, thinking, "If I do that, I won't have enough for me, or my family." I am sure though, after seeing Jesus bless and multiply the small portion of food given freely by the young boy, they would have wished they'd said YES to God. There were twelve baskets of food left over. Who do you think got to take them home? Maybe the disciples got some, but I think that little boy's mother would have been very happy that evening when her son returned home with an abundance of food in his hands.

Whatever you are facing, whatever mountain you have to climb, know that God can take your little and make it much.

MY GOD IS AN 'OIL JAR' FILLER

Day 37 TRACTION

There were days when we just hung onto that one thing from God to get us through, and then there were days like today where provision, support, opportunity to speak and further afield connections came in like a flood. We continued to receive provision from our garage bank, but today we also got the offer of a laptop for our ministry, had several pastors ring to inform us of their decision to support us, and further opportunities came to speak at churches around the country. Momentum was starting to build as we saw others choosing to step into our boat. No longer were we paddling like crazy alone, others were now onboard to join in the rowing to see us get to our destination on time.

> Therefore, since we are surrounded by such a huge crowd of witnesses to the life of faith, let us strip off every weight that slows us down, especially the sin that so easily trips us up. And let us run with endurance the race God has set before us.
> Hebrews 12:1 (NLT)

Momentum is defined as progress that increases in speed, and the impetus and speed of a moving object as it continues moving faster.

The secret to reaching your destination is to just keep moving. Don't stop, slow down, look back or let bumps in the road take you off track.

Momentum was happening in our life because we chose to continue to keep moving forward even though there were still bills to be paid, support and airfares to be raised, opportunities to be accepted and organisation yet to be finalized. Our daily language had to be, "We choose to get up and move forward." It was our only option.

MY GOD IS A GOD OF MOMENTUM

Day 38   STANDING IN WIDE OPEN SPACES

Being more of a night owl than a morning person, evenings have always been best for me to hear from God. For me, mornings were about getting myself up, organising the kids for school, tasks done and us all out the door on time. However, the further along I got into this two hundred day journey, the more sensitive I became to the presence of God being continually with me and around me and I was waking eager to hear from Him the moment I opened my eyes. Although I didn't do it religiously, I was grabbing my Bible as often as I could, to find and devour every morsel, knowing it would help carry me along this tightrope of a journey I was on.

"By entering through faith into what God has always wanted to do for us, set us right with Him, make us fit for Him, have it all together with God because of our Master Jesus. And that's not all, we throw open our doors to God and discover at the same moment, that He has already thrown open His door to us. We find ourselves standing where we always hoped we might stand, out in the wide open spaces of God's grace and glory, standing tall and shouting our praise." Romans 5:1-2 (MSG)

> We throw open our doors to God and discover at the same moment that He has already thrown open His door to us.
> Romans 5:1-2 (MSG)

Picture it, wide open spaces. Open fields, rolling hills that go on and on, further than the eye can see, reaching beyond our wildest imagination. When we stand in the middle of a wide open space we are literally surrounded on every side, every direction is encircled by God's grace and glory. A perfect representation of God, waiting with arms outstretched for us to run in to. Don't you just want to plant a big sloppy kiss on God's cheek right now and say a huge thank you for loving us this way?

How do we enter this open field? Only by the gateway of faith, can we step into what God has always wanted for us.

If nothing else happened today, this word was more than enough to carry me though, but God continued to pour oil into our jars through our unusual source, the garage store and someone gave me two movie tickets so I could take Belinda on a mother and daughter date.
As soon as we received those tickets I felt God was saying, "Enjoy this journey. Yes, keep doing what you are doing, keep moving forward, pushing through but take time to smell the roses, to go run in my wide open space, to feel the breeze blowing across your face and in your hair. Come on, put your feet in the water, splash in it and bask in my fields of grace for you."

MY GOD IS A GOD WHO HAS AN OPEN DOOR POLICY

Day 39 AMEN

"Thank you Lord for all things, for all the big things and all the small things you are doing in our life. Help me to not look at little things as little things. For to you God, all things are not counted as big or small but all things are counted as made possible in You. **Amen.**"

> To the angel of the church in Laodicea write: These are the words of the Amen, the faithful and true witness, the ruler of God's creation.
> Revelation 3:14 (NIV)

Prayer is our lifeline. Over the years when attacks from the enemy have come, we know the only way we have come through is because of prayer. Prayers we have prayed but mainly from the countless prayers our supporters and partners have prayed alongside us. Prayer is the backbone and the foundation for all we do. It's those prayers that have given us strength, favour and enduring passion to continue to do what we have been doing for the past eighteen years so far in Vietnam. Thank you, everyone who has, and continues to pray for us faithfully.

I called this section "Amen" for two reasons. The first reason is because my emphasis here is on prayer, but, secondly, because Amen is a powerful word. I wrote a sermon on Amen not so long ago and as I began to research this word in preparation for preaching, I found Amen has a lot of power.

Did you know Amen is actually one of the names for Jesus?

> For the Son of God, Jesus Christ, who was preached among you by us — by me (Paul), Silas and Timothy — was not "Yes" and "No," but in him it has always been "Yes." For no matter how many promises God has made, they are "Yes" in Christ. And so through Him, the "**Amen**" (emphasis added) is spoken by us to the glory of God. The Amen is Jesus Christ. 2 Corinthians 1:19 -20 (NIV)

As I was meditating on that word Amen, God began to speak to me about how we use this word. As most know, Amen means 'let it be so,' but God said to me, "Deb, do you realise when you are saying, 'Let it be so,' you are sealing what you say, throwing caution to the wind and letting it be as you say. When you say 'Amen' to me, you are saying, 'I take my hands off this now and fully trust in You, God, to deal with it and let it be so.'" When we say Amen, we must be intentional with this proclamation.

Today more finance came in which was always great, but I would have to say the greater thing that happened today was the phone call we received from a prayer group leader of a church we had spoken at, to say they would take it upon themselves to be vigilant in prayer for us every day.

Over the years, many wonderful people have come up to us and said, "Sorry I can't financially support you, I can only pray," but I would always answer them saying, "Don't ever say only pray. We would rather have thousands of people praying for us and a morsel of finance, than thousands of dollars and a morsel of prayer. As prayer often ended with Amen, we knew these people were praying, "Let it be so." Without the foundation of prayer, we have no sure base to build upon.

MY GOD IS THE GOD WE CAN COUNT ON TO 'LET IT BE SO'

Day 40   IT *IS* BUSINESS!

As part of the process of fundraising as a missionary, the usual deal goes something like this: Contact friends and pastors whom you have a relationship with, ask if you can send them your promotional pack for consideration of support, then if they show even a hint of interest, ask to meet with them so you can share your vision and hope they love it, and you. If indeed they do, and agree to financially support you, then the next thing you ask them is, to please refer you to their friends and other churches. Daunting right?

> The Spirit of the Lord is on me, because the Lord has anointed me to proclaim good news to the poor. He has sent me to bind up the brokenhearted, to proclaim freedom for the captives and release from darkness for the prisoners.
> Isaiah 61:1 (NIV)

It was definitely not my favourite activity. I personally found it very difficult putting my hand out for money. "Isn't there some other way God?" There wasn't, so I had no choice but to overcome the fear of possible rejection. For Paul on the other hand, it was no big deal. Being in sales all his life, he was not only used to cold calling people to get a sale but he was very successful at it until of course, we came to Tasmania. He'd happily ring up anyone and if people said no, it didn't faze him at all but for me if people said no, I would get very despondent. Paul had to lovingly encourage me on several occasions saying: "Who are you putting your trust in, God or man? People are not our source, God is! It's up to Him who supports us and who doesn't." I did finally get the message, eventually, slowly! I came to understand that the no we were getting was not a personal, "I don't like you" no, but more a "this is not where our church focus is at this moment" no, and I became ok with that.

With this issue dealt with, I still had a problem with what seemed like begging for money. I kept thinking, this is not business, this is ministry. It's ok to ask for money in business because business is not personal as it involves transactions between two parties. I chatted non-stop with God over it because I couldn't get it into my head that it was right. Eventually when I did take a breath long enough for God to get a word in, He gave me some enlightening revelation on this whole fundraising deal. He spoke very clearly to me and said, "Deb, this is business! This is my business, the business of saving lives, healing the broken hearted and setting captives free. You are not asking for money for you, you are asking people to partner with you to take care of my business and finance is one tool that is going to make this possible." "Wow God, that's right!" When I got hold of that insight, my whole perspective changed when asking people to partner with us. It became an opportunity for others to form a partnership, them, God and us to do His will in the nation of Vietnam.

With all that being said, it was still nice today to get an easy yes from someone who reminded us to send a promotional pack. "Hey, where's that support letter you were going to send out, I have been waiting for it so I can fill it in and start supporting you."

In life, we all want things the easy way don't we, but I have a feeling God allows some 'nos' along the way to keep our eyes firmly fixed on Him, the source of all our supply.

MY GOD IS A GOD WHO IS IN THE LIFE SAVING BUSINESS

Day 41 I WISH TO RECOMMEND

After sharing with you previously about the process of getting sponsorship, I am happy to say that today we received a nice injection of referrals and recommendations. I believe that came because of what I spoke on earlier, momentum. Keep moving forward and momentum will come.

Going to our mailbox these days had become quite an adventure. I would liken it to what Forrest Gump's mother once told him, (in the 1994 movie by the same name Forest Gump), "You never know what you are going to get!" Well, today we got a letter. No particular markings on it, no indication it was anything special. It definitely wasn't a bill, we were quite acquainted with those window faced envelopes. No, this was just a plain white envelope addressed to us.

> God's recommendation letter to us:
> "For it is not the one who commends himself who is approved, but the one whom the Lord commends."
> 2 Corinthians 10:18 (NIV)

On opening the letter, the first words that caught our attention were, "I wish to recommend." That alone was a boost to our spirits. What followed was a glowing report on us. Who we were, our character, our integrity, maturity in God and the belief in the vision we had. He finished his letter by saying, "I highly recommend you get behind this couple."

This is the kind of thing that builds your confidence and makes you feel valued. We all need a dose of that in our lives. Imagine how our day would change if someone took the time to send us an email, SMS, a Facebook or Twitter message or better still, called just to say, "I want to tell you how much I appreciate you and all you do." That recommendation letter came with twenty-one names. Twenty-one possible partners who had the opportunity to join us in God's business to see transformation in countless lives in Vietnam! Who wouldn't want to do that? Thank you Dermot for believing in us.

MY GOD IS A GOD WHO VALUES US

Day 42 - 43
GIVE OUR LIVES AWAY

It's the weekend. Saturday came and went but not uneventful as we continued to see more people stream into our garage for a sale. (You'd think there would be nothing left by now, wouldn't you)!

Then it was Sunday and we were always hungry for Sunday to come so we could glean from others who hear from God. I was especially eager today as we were having guest speakers. They were called Team Extreme. Team Extreme, even the name got me. Anyone doing anything extreme I wanted to hear from. Extreme is how we are to live. To me it speaks of throwing caution to the wind when it comes to trusting God, stepping out in His purposes and doing radical stuff for Him. This team had a whole production going on. They were a group of world class athletes who do extreme physical demonstrations, lifting weights, cars, crazy radical lifting, smashing bricks, tearing telephone books apart with their bare hands, (they even got Paul up to have a go at that one), as physical examples of pushing through tough stuff. As each one got up and did their thing, they shared their personal testimony of how God brought them through tough stuff, just as passionately as they had displayed in their natural physical ability. They spoke about the need to confront life's tough

> If you cling to your life, you will lose it; but if you give up your life for me, you will find it.
> Matthew 10:39 (NLT)

issues head on as a motivation to push through and become all we are destined to be. Extreme physical measure, extreme passionate gratefulness to God for all He does and extreme worship to the only One who saves.

Be holy, spend time in the Word and worship, be a giver, give your life away, discover your spiritual gifts and be totally obedient. I think what they were really saying was, "Just say YES to God."

Give our lives away. Why not, I say! We need to realise our lives are much more productive in God's hands anyway. Be extreme, throw caution to the wind and let God, our extreme God breath on us to do the radical.

While I was processing just how incredibly extreme God has been with us so far, people started walking up to us and putting pledge notes for support and money into our hands. You have to think about this. We were not the speakers yet God was directing people to us. That's our radical extreme God!

I am more than happy to give my life away. What about you?

MY GOD IS A GOD WHO DESERVES OUR EXTREME OBEDIENCE.

Day 44 - 45 THE WIND IN OUR SAILS

It was a nice surprise to see how dramatically our Vietnam account had grown in just a few short months and we were also pleased to be watching our pile of debt go down, little by little. Finally we were moving closer to financial freedom and further away from the grip of the debt that had ensnared us over the past six years. For a time our boat was sailing on smoother waters and the rowing was becoming less difficult. It was great to take a breather from pushing against such strong winds and just allow God to gently blow on the sails to carry us forward.

This didn't mean all the negative stuff just dropped off. We knew there were still rough seas ahead to conquer, including dealing with the rest of the debt accumulated from our crippling business, but regardless of how high the waves got, we determined to stay in the boat, because it was being in the boat that kept us from going under. It was in the boat, we learnt life lessons. It was in the boat, God took the negative of that business and used it to become the very thing to build us, grow us and teach us total dependence on Him. Staying planted in that boat made us richer than we had ever been in our whole lives. We are forever grateful for this baptism of fiery growth because without it, we would not be the people we are today.

> I am the vine; you are the branches. If you remain in me and I in you, you will bear much fruit.
> John 15:5 (NIV)

These two days were gold, as God had me meditating on all He had done in us through the fire. I can't stress enough, the power of staying in the boat.

MY GOD IS A GOD WHO TEACHES GREAT LESSONS IN HIS LIFEBOAT

Day 46
IT'S ALL IN A DAY'S WORK

Yeek! The insurance bill is due.

God's diary is not like ours, putting appointments in for the week or the following day. No, God's diary is one of yesterday, today and forever. He has a lifetime organised for you and me. Although He checks it daily, He is already well prepared.

God: "Oh yes, today Paul and Deb are going to be needing money for their insurance bill. They will be chatting with me about it this morning in their usual fashion asking me how on earth will it be paid, but I know how in Heaven, it will be done. I've got the provision ready and I can't wait to see their faces when it comes!"

Paul and Me: "God, you know we have this insurance bill due today, but we have no idea how it will be paid. Please, can you show us what we need to do and we thank you for your provision."

> Giving thanks is the sacrifice that honors me, and I will surely save all who obey me.
> Psalm 50:23 (GNT)

Within hours of us praying, a lady came and bought our two tubs chairs for the price of our car insurance. "Wow God, you are so astounding. Every single day we are amazed by You."

I believe there are two things God expects of us as His children. One, is for us to have abandoned faith, and two, always have a heart of gratitude remembering He never leaves us or forsakes us, and is well aware of our needs and always has been, even before they were ever on the map.

What He does for us is just all in a day's work to Him, but He is motivated by two key ingredients. Abandoned faith and gratitude.

MY GOD IS A GOD WHO BY OUR FAITH AND GRATITUDE WILL ASTOUND US

Day 47
WHAT LANGUAGE ARE YOU SPEAKING?

There were two major things we had to accomplish to get to our promised land. One, I had to complete a TESOL (Course to Teach English to

Speakers of Other Languages) course, and secondly, both Paul and I, needed to attend World Harvest Institute (Our mission training course). Both required time and finance!

Doing TESOL was a big faith step for me because it meant study. Schooling had not been my best achievement in life, having left after the completion of grade 10.

I will never forget that first TESOL lesson. On arrival each one of us had to introduce ourselves to the class. "Hi, I am Tom, I am a school teacher and have a teaching degree, and a this and that degree." "Hello, my name is Mary and I am a University lecturer with a zillion years experience." "Hi, my name is Julie and I have been teaching English for several years overseas." "Hi, I am John and I have a teaching degree and seven years overseas experience," and around the classroom it went with similar stories. Then it was my turn. "Hi, I'm Deb and I work in a bank and I have no experience teaching."

Yep, that's me! No degree, no higher education, no experience and the best school day of my life, was the day I left.

That first TESOL lesson was interesting to say the least. They began speaking in a language I had never heard before, 'past tense continuous, simple present, present progressive.' What's that? Everyone was nodding, and agreeing to what was being taught so I thought I better nod too, but I had no idea what I was agreeing to. Inside I was crying out to God to help me and thinking what on earth am I doing here! I thought this would be easy, I know English. Maybe it was something taught after I left school!

My mind went into a backflip and everything within me wanted to run out that door, but because I was sure this was something God had told me to do, I would, with God's help, learn to understand this new fandangled version of English and learn I did. Me and God not only got through it, but ended up doing very well. I guess God has a reputation to live up to.

When we journey with God on a new unknown path, get ready to be surprised how God will answer. Don't box Him in thinking money alone is the solution to everything. It may just come in the form of supernatural skill.

> For we are God's [own] handiwork (His workmanship), recreated in Christ Jesus, [born anew] that we may do those good works that God predestined (planned beforehand) for us [taking paths which He prepared ahead of time], that we should walk in them [living the good life which He prearranged and made ready for us to live].
> Ephesians 2:10 (AMP)

MY GOD IS THE GOD WHO GIVES KNOWLEDGE AND ABILITY FOR THE TASK

Day 48 BROUGHT BEFORE LEADERS

Who are we that we should be endorsed and supported by our church's State President?

Proverbs 22:29 (NKJV) says, "Do you see a man who excels in his work? He will stand before kings; He will not stand before unknown men."

Yes, we had a great relationship with our State President. However, his decision to endorse and support us was not based on our friendship, but on what he saw in us, our character and diligence. Perfect we were not, but we highly valued, being known as people of good character and diligence, to the best of our ability.

Receiving a phone call, to further confirming support from the State on this day was amazing. It further cemented God's validation of our call.

> May the favor of the Lord our God rest on us; establish the work of our hands for us—yes, establish the work of our hands.
> Psalm 90:17 (NIV)

When we are close to the King of Kings, He will have us walking with kings.

MY GOD IS A GOD WHO SITS US AT HIS TABLE

Day 49
DON'T DESPISE THE SMALL BEGINNINGS

We had great expectations today because we needed over one thousand dollars. What did God have up His sleeve for us today?

We jumped onto the computer and there it was, 'You've Got Mail.' There was an email from a friend who had given us the promise of support. We were eager to see what her pledge amount was going to be. Could it be the answer to our thousand dollar need?

"I want to send you twenty dollars."

How would you look at that twenty dollars in the midst of the numerous dollars needed for the day? If twenty dollars were all that came in despite needing so much more, what would be your response? "God, that isn't enough. God, just twenty dollars? God, didn't you hear me when I said we needed over thousand dollars today?" Or would you say, "God, you are so amazing, you spoke to someone in another state to give of the little they have to be a blessing to us today. Thank you so much for the twenty dollars. Please, Lord, do what needs to be done with that twenty dollars and we trust you for the rest."

Thankfully, we prayed the latter. As I said in Day 46, thankfulness moves the heart of God. It was easy for us to pray that prayer because we just knew in our hearts God was going provide the thousand dollars. You see something supernatural was happening in us during this two hundred day walk. The path we were on was no natural path. It is impossible to fully articulate in words the journeying God had us on, but we felt like we were walking with Him on the outskirts of heaven as we saw Him do miracle after miracle for us.

After that prayer of thanksgiving for the twenty dollars, abundance began to pour in. We got a phone call about our big ticket item we had for sale, the tent, and before we knew it those people were on our doorstep with cash in hand. Before they left, they had purchased not only the tent but also several other items we had for sale. As they were leaving, the owners of the house we were staying in also came to buy of our wares. By lunchtime we had one thousand and two hundred dollars in our hands!

And it didn't stop there. Paul also got a free airfare to Sydney to begin World Harvest Institute and we were able to pay off all the course fees in plenty of time before he commenced.

> And now just as you trusted Christ to save you, trust Him, too, for each day's problems; live in vital union with Him. Let your roots grow down into Him and draw up nourishment from Him. See that you go on growing in the Lord, and become strong and vigorous in the truth you were taught. Let your lives overflow with joy and thanksgiving for all He has done.
> Colossians 2:6-7 (TLB)

I am writing this to the best of my ability to give you a glimpse of just how God works and will work for you when you just step out of your boat and get into His.

MY GOD IS A GOD WHO DESIRES US TO KNOW HIM DEEPER, WALK WITH HIM CLOSER AND THANK HIM FOR ALL HE HAD DONE

Day 50 LETTERS FROM THE APOSTLE PAUL

> I, Paul, have been called and sent by Jesus, the Messiah, according to God's plan, along with my friend Sosthenes. I send this letter to you in God's church at Corinth, believers cleaned up by Jesus and set apart for a God-filled life. I include in my greeting all who call out to Jesus, wherever they live. He's their Master as well as ours! May all the gifts and benefits that come from God our Father, and the Master, Jesus Christ, be yours. Every time I think of you—and I think of you often!—I thank God for your lives of free and open access to God, given by Jesus. There's no end to what has happened in you—it's beyond speech, beyond knowledge. The evidence of Christ has been clearly verified in your lives. Just think—you don't need a thing, you've got it all! All God's gifts are right in front of you as you wait expectantly for our Master Jesus to arrive on the scene for the Finale. And not only that, but God himself is right alongside to keep you steady and on track until things are all wrapped up by Jesus. God, who got you started in this spiritual adventure, shares with us the life of his Son and our Master Jesus. He will never give up on you. Never forget that. 1 Corinthians 1:1-9 (MSG)

It was Sunday, we walked into a church all geared up to speak about our vision with both excitement and nervous anticipation. Is this church going to get behind us? Although we were full of passion, the vision we had was still in its embryonic stage.

It was so encouraging to have the leader of the church's missions department come straight up to us after we spoke to encourage us. "I just want you to know, not only are we going to support you but we are going to be your biggest fans. We are going to write to you and encourage you while you serve on the field. We believe in you and we want you to know we are championing your cause." Other members of the congregation also came up to us and encouraged us, prayed with us, spoke words over us and also promised to write.

We were going to get letters from encouragers, our cheer squad who would raise a banner for us in the grandstand with our names on it saying, "We love you, we believe in you and you are going to win." This put a huge smile on our faces and joy in our hearts.

Don't ever doubt that God is championing your cause. His cause for you!

Take a moment and put your name to 1 Corinthians 1:1-9.

I, your *encourager/supporter* have been called and sent by Jesus, the Messiah, according to God's plan, along with my friend *other encouragers/supporters.* I send this letter to you **Deb** in God's church, **you Deb,** cleaned up by Jesus and set apart for a God-filled life. I include in my greeting all who call out to Jesus, wherever they live. He's their Master as well as ours! May all the gifts and benefits that come from God our Father, and the Master, Jesus Christ, be yours **Deb**. Every time I think of you **Deb**—and I think of you often!—I thank God for your life **Deb** free and open access to God, given by Jesus. There's no end to what has happened in you **Deb**—it's beyond speech, beyond knowledge. The evidence of Christ has been clearly verified in your life **Deb**. Just think **Deb**—you don't need a thing, you've got it all! All God's gifts are right in front of you as you wait expectantly for our Master Jesus to arrive on the scene for the Finale. And not only that, but God himself is right alongside to keep you steady and on track until things are all wrapped up by Jesus. God, who got you started in this spiritual adventure, shares with you the life of his Son and your Master Jesus. He will never give up on you **Deb**. Never forget that.

You will notice a few things in this scripture that are vital tools to remember. Besides the obvious that God is with us, has set everything in place for us and given us encouragement and a fan club, Paul wants to remind us when He states, "Cleaned up by Jesus," that God is not looking for perfect people, or ones who have it all together, but simply ones who have been cleaned up by Jesus. If it were the perfect or the all together people He chose, I would still be sitting in the back of the classroom, as I would never have made the grade. I am chosen simply because I am totally cleansed through the shed blood of Jesus Christ and His mercy and grace have been extended to me. Secondly, when Paul states, "There is no end to what has happened to you, it's beyond speech," what He is saying is, "Let your messes becomes your message to the glory of God. He uses it all."

> May our Lord Jesus Christ himself and God our Father, who loved us and by his grace gave us eternal encouragement and good hope, encourage your hearts and strengthen you in every good deed and word.
> 2 Thessalonians 2: 16-17 (NIV)

Letters from home, from our fans, became life-blood to us on the field in those difficult early years. On the days we felt alone, discouraged or just worn out, it was those letters that lifted us up. The words may have only said, "Hello, we are praying and thinking of you," but they shouted out loud, "We champion you, we love you, you are going to win and we are your biggest fans."

MY GOD IS A GOD WHO CHAMPIONS ME FROM THE GRANDSTAND

Day 51 EVERY DROP OF DEW

God we still have a long way to go to get all our support! How about a big chunk today God? Let's fast track this support-raising thing. We checked our emails? No, no emails today. We looked out the window to see if anybody was coming around to buy what was left of our personal gear. No, no one. Not even a single person on the street. The phone didn't even ring. "Well God, I know you will do something, don't know what that something is, but whatever it is, it will be our day 51 miracle."

It was late in the day when we heard that all familiar sound of the postman's motorbike stop at our mailbox. Whenever our family heard that sound, everyone would jump up and say, "It's my turn to get the mail."

> May God give you heaven's dew and earth's richness, an abundance of grain and new wine.
> Genesis 27:28 (NIV)

Would it be a windowed envelope or a hand written letter of promise? Yes, a non-windowed version and it's from a church. Great, how much? The first thing we did was to scan the letter for numbers but there were none, so we reread the letter to see what it actually was saying to us. "We will support you but cannot give you an amount yet. We will let you know soon."

The promise of support! Lord, we asked for a downpour, but you gave us a dewdrop. However, we thank you for that drop of dew you released into our laps today. God keep our eyes on you, the one who holds every drop of water and disperses it as you see fit. I know that every single drop of dew will eventually become a flowing river and that river will be more than enough water to sustain my family for as long as we needed it to.

MY GOD IS THE GOD OF EVERY DROP OF RAIN

Day 52 - 53
SEVEN LOAVES, A FEW FISH AND FOUR THOUSAND MEN

I was awoken by God these two mornings, with my mind filled with the destiny, and plans He has for Vietnam. Unique, specifically laid out plans, for us to be part of. It overwhelmed me because Vietnam was a country of over seventy million people in 1997, (over ninety million in 2016), with insurmountable needs, both physically and spiritually.

In the natural, I couldn't imagine how we could even meet a fraction of this huge population's needs. I went to the only place that would have an answer for me, His Word! I opened my Bible and began flicking through the pages until my eyes fell on a text heading in Matthew 15:32-39 (NLT) called "Jesus Feeds Four Thousand."

> Jesus said, "I feel sorry for these people. They have been here with me for three days and have nothing left to eat. I don't want to send them away hungry, or they will faint along the way." The disciples replied "Where would we get enough food here in the wilderness for such a huge crowd?"

Yes, that's what I was thinking too, God. "Where are we going to get enough skill, talent, time, money and resource, to 'feed' this huge crowd in Vietnam the way you are showing me we will?

> Jesus said, "How much bread do you have?"
> Disciples: "Seven loaves, and a few small fish."

Jesus to me: "What is in your hands now?"
Deb: "Lord, I have a passion, I can speak, I can teach, I can play music, but is that going to be enough?"

> Jesus said to his disciples: "Sit everyone down, I will take these loaves and fish and thank God for them, then I will break them into pieces and then you will distribute them to the crowd."

Jesus to me: "Deb, sit down a minute. Now give me what you have. I am lifting it up to my Father and thanking Him for what He has given you. I will then break it into as many pieces as necessary, multiplying it for you to distribute to my people in Vietnam."

The crowd ate and seven large baskets of leftover food were picked up. There were four thousand men that day plus women and children.

> Indeed I will greatly bless you, and I will greatly multiply your seed as the stars of the heavens and as the sand which is on the seashore; and your seed shall possess the gate of their enemies.
> Genesis 22:17 (NASB)

Jesus to me: "Deb, I am more than enough for you. Give me what you have, and watch what I will do with it."

The enemy will always tell you that you are not good enough, don't have what it takes or couldn't possibly do what God has in mind for you to do, but God says, "Not only have I chosen you, equipped you and appointed you, I will multiply what you do for generations."

MY GOD IS A GOD WHO MULTIPLIES THE ORDINARY TO MAKE IT EXTRA ORDINARY

Day 54 HERITAGE

I loved listening to my grandmother tell me stories of her life growing up in England. She spoke with such passion that it brought to life every event. She talked about how she loved watching her brothers and their friends play cricket in the back narrow laneways and about having to walk through deep snow to get to school, dragging her younger siblings behind her. More than anything else though, she loved to tell me about her mother, my great grandmother, who would gather all the seven children around the fireplace after dinner to share of her own past but also to listen to stories from the Bible, about the Lord and His goodness.

Grandma also told me of the many struggles they often faced having to feed such a large family on so little money. With nine mouths to feed during the season of World War 1, life was difficult, yet God would always provide, sometimes miraculously. I will never forget the time she told me about the day they had no food at all in the house. Nothing. It was dinnertime, but her mother, my great- grandmother, told the children to set the table and prepare for dinner. As they began putting plates around the table, my grandmother said to her mother, "What will we eat?" And with incredible faith, my great-grandmother said to her, "God will provide." She beckoned everyone to sit down and as they sat down at a table laden with empty plates, they bowed their heads and my great grandmother prayed to God thanking Him for what He would bring.

My great-grandmother used to make socks to sell for extra income because her husband, my great-grandfather, earned very little in the English mines. These socks were a God-send for this family as it made the difference between eating and starving. As with any normal sales transaction, people would come, put their order in and then pay on the day they received their goods.

It seems there were no orders this week, which meant no money was available to buy the much needed food to feed her large family. This didn't phase my God fearing great grandmother as she by faith prepared her meal table this day, as if she had a feast.

As they finished praying for their dinner, even though there was no food at all, a knock came on the door. "Hello, I believe you make socks. I know this may seem strange, but would you mind if we pay you up front for these socks and pick them up when you are done?"

Can you imagine the looks on all those children's faces? You had better believe how that built faith in my grandmother and her siblings, and not just on this occasion, but the many others they saw come into their home because of a praying mother.

We also had days like my grandmother's, when we didn't know where today's food was going to come from, and today was one of those days. There were only four in our family, but still each day meant we needed faith to believe in God's provision.

Several months before this two hundred day journey, we had a prophesy spoken over us and the main point of it said, "There is an enlarging process going on in you right now, it's like God is saying, I'm going to kick out the walls a bit further and I am going to enlarge you a bit more and there is a reason for that."

> Now faith is the confidence in what we hope for and assurance about what we do not see.
> Hebrews 11:1 (NIV)

Walking through this every day, step by step, morsel by morsel, faith stretching journey was definitely kicking out some walls and we were certainly being enlarged. In our past affluent life, trusting God was from the safe confines of a secure comfort zone, but now, those walls of comfort had been kicked right out and we were at a place where there was nothing to hold onto but God.

The good news is, the same God my great-grandmother prayed to, is the same God we pray to. Today we also bowed our heads, asked God for His provision, thanking Him for what He would bring, and today, we too had our own knock on the door.

**MY GOD IS A GOD WHO BLESSES
FROM GENERATION TO GENERATION**

Day 55
WHEN SHUT DOORS SWING WIDE OPEN

Sometimes we can look at a shut door and say, "That door is shut forever", so we give up on it. However, not all closed doors are permanently locked. Some are only closed for a season.

When we approach the door of a new idea, a great strategy or a brilliant concept, we say to ourselves, "This is so good, perfect in fact, that we will be able to walk straight in," but sometimes try as we might, push on it, bang on it, try turning the handle numerous times, the door remains tightly sealed with no sign of it ever opening and we are left wondering why. "Why on earth when this masterminded inspiration makes so much sense, doesn't it work? Why isn't it opening?"

However, as we are not ones to give up so easily, because we are sure it is a God idea we go back to that door once again. At first we try the pushing on it weekly, then monthly, and maybe if we are really stubborn, we will go back to it yearly until finally we say, "OK God, I give up, the door is shut, you've locked it and obviously thrown away the key. I was sure it was Your idea but because it hasn't opened thus far, I am not sure anymore."

Then one day, when you are least expecting it, when you thought it was all over, you see that sealed, bolted door that you had finally put behind you, not just creak open slightly but swing wide open and you realise, now is the right time. Then, if you are smart enough, you will thank God it didn't open beforehand. That 'great idea' not only becomes a reality, but also turns out much better that you had planned and God gets the glory.

This was our experience with a simple idea we had to raise funds. At the beginning of the year, before we had begun our serious journey of preparation for Vietnam, we were handed boxes of Vietnamese tablecloths, souvenirs, and other beautiful items from that same pastor who had spoken into our lives about the nation of Vietnam at the mission's summit. He was generous enough to allow us to purchase them at cost price but pay for them once we started selling the products. There was a lot of money sitting in those boxes and we needed money. We thought this was surely a God idea so He will open all the doors we need to sell so we can make a decent profit and get out of debt quickly. People are bound to want to buy these amazing, beautiful and saleable items. This is going to be easy money!

Both Paul and I were great salespeople, so we thought once we open our mouths, all these items would sell in a flash, after all, look at our garage sale phenomenon, but no matter how creative our marketing or even how much people expressed their interest or remarked on the lovely merchandise, no one was buying. No one! For months we tried, every conceivable way, but at each attempt, we came up empty.

And the scenario began, "But God, but, but, but…" Yet all the 'buts' in the world had not unlocked that door over those proceeding months. It didn't make sense. Everything lined up. We needed money. This makes money. They were products from Vietnam so what better items could we have had in our hands for sale than those from the nation God was sending us to? "What part of this scenario doesn't make sense to you God?" Nevertheless, no matter how much we kicked, pushed or banged on that door it was not budging. We were looking at a door that was sealed with both bolts and chains so we packed the boxes up and put them into storage.

Today, ten months after putting that great idea to bed, the 'all of a sudden' took place for us. An email came in from the organisation which had given us the boxes of handicrafts, and in that message they wrote to say they had decided not to charge us for all those goods but instead, give them to us so we could use the money to get ourselves to Vietnam.

As we read this news, our hearts jumped. I can't explain it, but a shift happened in our spirits and we just knew God was handing us the key to unlock the door for those items to finally sell and sell they did. What unraveled over the following months was miraculous, which I will share with you soon.

When Martha heard that Jesus was coming, she went out to meet him, but Mary stayed at home. "Lord," Martha said to Jesus, "If you had been here (earlier), my brother would not have died." Then Jesus said, "Did I not tell you that if you believed, you would see the glory of God?" John 11:20-21, 40 (NIV)

> There is a time for everything, and a season for every activity under the heavens:
> Ecclesiastes 3:1 (NIV)

Our human response to an unrealised opportunity is, "God, if only you had come earlier," and His answer is always, "I intended to answer you. Did I not tell you that if you believe, you will see the glory of God?"

You may say, this story of Lazarus, Martha's brother, is an extreme example to compare to our Vietnamese materials, but the principle is the same. God must be glorified in our journey. It's His blueprint for our life, not our blueprint for Him.

The key to all we do in serving God is to keep the main thing the main thing. For the glory be to Him and Him alone.

MY GOD IS THE GOD TO WHOM ALL GLORY BE GIVEN

Day 56 FAITH OF A MUSTARD SEED

Matthew 17:20 tells us that if we have even just 'grain sized faith', He will do mighty things.

I am so grateful that God only requires a mustard seed of faith from us to move even the greatest of mountains, mountains in our life, which seem impossible for us to conquer. I asked God the question, "Why do You require only a tiny morsel of faith from us to do our seemingly monumental unachievable requests?" His answer was simple, "Deb, I know so well your human frailty. The comparison between what you can believe for, compared to what I can do, is incomparable. My ability is infinite. My capability compared to your faith ability is immeasurable but with that little you have, I am more than able to do what is needed to be done." Isn't God amazing?

> You don't have enough faith," Jesus told them. "I tell you the truth, if you had faith even as small as a mustard seed, you could say to this mountain, 'Move from here to there,' and it would move. Nothing would be impossible."
> Matthew 17:20 (NLT)

When we began our debt-busting journey, the mountain was so big, we could not see any way of achieving our goal of ridding this monster from our lives before moving onto our next season. All we knew to do was offer up our mustard seed of faith to God and begin to move forward, doing what we could in the natural and trust God to move the mountain that was in front of us into the sea.

Today, we got to see that mountain get thrown deep into the oceanic abyss. Today, the last of our business debt was paid. Unbelievable, total relief, and our complete gratitude to God was beyond words. God really does move mountains!

We could now take a rest for a little while. Not a rest from faith, moving forward or trusting God, but a 'come away with me and celebrate the victory' rest. A time to sit back, reflect and soak in the wonder of God, thanking Him for all He has done so far on this journey.

MY GOD IS A GOD WHO CRUMBLES MOUNTAINS

Day 57
DON'T YOU SEE I AM DOING A NEW THING?

With our business debt behind us, the weight lifted off us; we felt lightness in our whole being! I don't know how else to describe it but it was like we were floating on air. However, because we had been in the boxing ring with this monster for so long, it almost felt strange not to be fighting with it anymore. Good strange, but strange all the same. Six years of wrestling to overcome what began as a good investment, but that had turned into a nightmare, was now finally over, and it felt a little weird.

When you have been trusting for a mountain to move for such a long time, it is easy to still have that mountain sitting in your mind long after it has been thrust into the sea. You have to also make a conscious mind shift that your mountain truly has left the building. Don't fear the mountain will return. The enemy will tell you it is not really gone or it is bound to come back but what God has done, is done!

> Forget the former things; do not dwell on the past. See, I am doing a new thing!
> Isaiah 43: 18-19a (NIV)

Through it all; the pain, the challenges, the faith and disbelief, we got to know God in a greater way and for that, we wouldn't change a thing. Do we want to go through it again, ah that would be, "No," but through the struggle, came much gain for us personally. It forged in us a stronger character, greater trust, a deeper love for our amazing God and a bigger, 'I can do all things through Christ that strengthens me' mindset that molded us for His long term purposes. Again, I can say with conviction, we wouldn't change a thing.

Today was also Sunday and we were speaking at a church. On our arrival we were ushered to the front. Yep, we got to sit right up the front. How nice! When we were called to the platform, we were welcomed as the missionaries to Vietnam. My first thought was, our title has changed. The old is now behind us, and the new is upon us. We shared our vision and as we stepped off that platform we also stepped into our new chapter.

This church totally embraced us and before we left we were assured of their support. We were handed an envelope by a lady at the church who said, "This is a love offering for you from the church," and for the first time, we could look at money without the words 'business debt' written all over it. This would be going into our Vietnam account!

MY GOD IS A GOD WHO GRADUATES US

Day 58
THE LESSONS YOU LEARN ARE TO GIVE AWAY

We had dinner plans this evening with a great couple. They had initiated the get together and we were more than happy to catch up and glean from such seemingly successful, well to do people whom we saw as a real example of faith.

We had no sooner sat down to eat when they began to pour out their hearts to us. They shared about their overwhelming business debt but also how they had a desire to serve God in a greater way. Sound familiar? It certainly did to us.

> Now I want you to know, brothers and sisters, that what has happened to me has actually served to advance the gospel.
> Philippians 1:12 (NIV)

When God takes you through something, be assured He will call on you to use your testimony for others. This is our responsibility. It is for others to glean from, to be healed through or to be used as catalysts for them to start moving towards their own destiny, and this my friends, is why I am writing this book! It is for you!

Only we could minister into this situation, because we had been there. The miracle in my book today was seeing God use the fruit He had put into us, go forth and multiply to serve others.

MY GOD IS GLORIFIED IN OUR TESTIMONY

Day 59
HE DETERMINES THE NUMBER OF THE STARS

Before starting to write about day 59, I picked up an old journal of mine, one of many journals I have written, and started reading the first entry. It began with me writing down Psalm 147:4 (NIV), "He determines the number of the stars and calls each one by name."

On that particular day I had been talking to God about how I was always concerned about numbers. I have this much, so I can do this, I need that much to be able to do that, but after reading Psalm 147:4 I was quickly reminded of who the determiner of numbers is, God, and just how detailed He is. He is the counter of every dollar, the weigher of every need, the distributor of every resource and keeper of each moment of time. There is nothing that misses the eye of God.

> He determines the number of the stars and calls each one by name.
> Psalm 147:4 (NIV)

After reading this gold nugget, I was encouraged to find on returning to the journal I am writing my two hundred days experience from, that on day 59 I wrote, "There is enough for all we need so why should I be concerned, God is higher, He is, and has enough!"

Be encouraged. Keep moving. Keep saying YES to God no matter what. God's got every single element covered. If He is able to count the numerous stars in the heavens and give each and every single one of them a name, He can surely deliver to your days; finance, time, words, resource, whatever it is you need and it will be tailor made just for you.

I am definitely cheering for you and our number determiner, Almighty God, and His host of angels are also cheering for you shouting loud, "Keep going!"

MY GOD IS THE ULTIMATE ACCOUNTANT

Day 60   ONE BODY, MANY PARTS

A church cannot run effectively with just a pastor, a business doesn't operate successfully solely with a boss, a factory won't function with only the supervisor and a missionary cannot go to a field without people behind them. Success is only achieved when it is done with a team. We cannot believe that any mission or business can be accomplished on the strengths of just one person. Behind every front man doing great exploits there is a team of extraordinary people working, sometimes out front, but more often than not, behind the scenes, and without them, it would be like an eight cylinder car running on just two of those cylinders. Eventually the motor would begin to strain and possibly, stop working altogether.

Gathering partners to take this journey with us was vital. We needed a team for prayer support, correspondence and encouragement, and financial support. As we became more known by people throughout the state and beyond, we were gaining such a team around us to do just that.

Today, a good friend offered their services to become our long distant assistant. Wow, I hadn't even thought about that one. She said, "I will handle all your incoming and outgoing mail and be the go-to person for you." As I said before, when we started our ministry, most people wrote letters, very few had email and as for Instragram and Facebook, they were non-existent. Our wonderful friend even offered to look after our cat!

> For we are co-workers in God's service; you are God's field, God's building.
> 1 Corinthians 3:9 (NIV)

Every day, every single day, I continued to get something from God to say, "I am determining those numbers for you, I have everything covered for you Deb."

What is your call, what is your passion? Is it to start a business, change jobs, change locations, go back to school, learn a new skill, create something, write a book, write a song, start a church, become a doctor, a pastor, get up on that stage and be part of the music team, I could name a hundred or more things but whatever it is, know that God put that DNA inside of you so you can be sure, that what He has done, and is doing for us, He will also do for you!

MY GOD IS A TEAM PLAYER

Day 61 TWO MONTHS TODAY

It has been two months, or sixty-one days, since I made a pact with God, asking Him to do something each day to show He was guiding us to our destined future and so far, He has not disappointed me. He continues to surprise and amaze me through the big and small gifts He has presented in each and every day just as He said He would do.

> Look straight ahead, and fix your eyes on what lies before you.
> Proverbs 4:25 (NLT)

Today brought the gift of further giving. More and more

people were starting to sow into our ministry now, which meant our Vietnam account was looking very healthy. Sometimes when people gave us money, they'd say, "This is for your ministry in Vietnam, but if you need to, you can use it now." It was always tempting to use it for the now because the now would often lure us, justifying the need to spend it but we knew that unless we continued to pour into the then, our focus would be more directed on the now, leaving a deficit in our then. We made the choice that if any funds came to us for ministry, even if it was offered to use for now, we would pour it into the then, trusting God He had the now sorted, and sorted He always did.

Stay committed to the whole journey package, and see the faithfulness of God.

MY GOD IS THE GOD OF NOW RIGHT THROUGH TO THEN

Day 62 IT'S NOT ALL GOING TO BE ROSY!

If you have actually got up from that chair of indecision and begun moving towards your destiny, for sure you would have come across obstacles, distractions, negative comments and unexpected hurdles. If not, you are not living. It is only natural that these things will come. This is not a sign you are going the wrong way or doing something wrong. It simply means, stuff happens. That's it. However, knowing God and knowing all things work together for good, we can be confident that everything will still come together as we look to God in the midst of that stuff.

Today was one of those days. We received news that there would not be any government funding for us while we did our nine-week mission training course, and for icing on that cake, we got an unexpected bill from the accountant for $1000. My first response was, fantastic… not! Nine weeks with absolutely no funding at all for four people to live, pay for travel, board, resources and anything else that came up in between.

There had been so many up days of late, that it took me by surprise when our day started out with these stuff happens events, but despite my discouragement, my momentum of trust and confidence in God was continuing to grow stronger and I just knew in my heart that today, God would still have, or do, something for me and today, was all I needed to be concerned with.

> The light shines in the darkness, and the darkness has not overcome it.
> John 1:5 (NIV)

That afternoon we took the kids out to the shops and while we were there, Paul ducked over to the post office. As he was leaving he bumped into a lady from our church, a lady who only came occasionally. "I've been trying to catch up with you, I want to support you, God's been speaking to me to support you." I was so excited to hear that news and even more so when we arrived home to see a card and twenty-five dollars left in an envelope from her at our front door.

The widows mite of twenty-five dollars didn't come close to the support needed for the nine weeks, and a $1,000 bill, but it didn't matter because God had turned up to say I am is still working when stuff happens.

We must never forget to appreciate the little things God does for us, not just the big things.

**MY GOD'S SMALLEST LIGHT
WILL OUTSTRIP ANY DARKNESS**

Day 63 CATCH AND RELEASE

We now had some idea of when we would depart the shores of our beloved country, Australia to go to our new home in Vietnam, but there was a chasm of time in the middle we needed to journey through these two sureties. This place was called the unknown. We had to trust God in this in between time for every little detail of the walk before us. The new, the unfamiliar, and the mysterious that was to come.

Attending World Harvest Institute in Sydney would take us to a city well known to us in some ways, but at the same time, so unfamiliar. Just two hours south of our hometown Newcastle, we travelled there often to enjoy the sites and buzz of one of the most famous cities in the world. However, although a road well travelled by us on many occasions, we had very few personal connections there.

It was also made very clear to us from all our sponsoring churches that funds for serving in Vietnam would only start once we were at the stage of leaving and not beforehand. This was normal practice for any church and we completely understood their stance. So with nine weeks of training ahead of us, no financial support while studying and no idea where we would stay, it once again brought us to our knees. And once again, God showed up.

We had been standing on one mountain, looking at the mountain beyond and the ravine in between seemingly had no bridge. We had been so busy looking at the depth of this ravine; where to stay, how to eat, who to connect with, that we had forgotten to look above the mountain tops to see how God was busily building the much needed bridge behind the scenes.

One of the board members of our church who was just happening to catch up with Paul later on in the day, gave Paul the opportunity to mention the need to start planning our Sydney leg.

> But Jesus answered them, My Father has worked [even] until now, [He has never ceased working; He is still working] and I, too, must be at [divine] work.
> John 5:17 (AMP)

As Paul began to share our situation with our good friend and board member, Dave, he said, "Well, actually one of the reasons I wanted to catch up with you today was to let you know that the board have decided to release all the money we have saved up for you, early. You will have it by the time you reach Sydney."

Hebrews 4:12 (NIV) says, "God's word is alive and active." We need to believe in our eternally alive, mobile God, who doesn't even take a catnap.

And before we lay our head on the pillow that night, we had received yet another promise of support from people we had only met once.

MY GOD IS A GOD WHO DOESN'T TAKE A SIESTA

Day 64 HEAVEN'S CONFIRMATION

Today - 23rd November, 1997, four days prior to Paul leaving for Sydney and 20 days before the kids and I would join him.

An excerpt from a very long prophesy we received this day.

The Lord would say to you, Paul and Deb, He has led you by His Spirit to the decisions you have taken. The Holy Spirit is leading you out of this place just as He lead Abraham and led him on to be a sojourner in a way that he did not know what was going to happen and all that would be involved. The glory cloud has moved on for your life, your provision and your prosperity, your blessing, your anointing, everything you need as a family is, as you walk under the glory cloud.

Although we should not hang our hat on prophesies, they definitely give us a faith boost when it confirms something that is happening in our life. This was the case for us as we stood on the edge of the springboard that was about to launch us out into the depths. It was the last Sunday in our church as a family and as we stood there receiving this word, a sense of finality came upon us. There was no turning back.

> But when He, the Spirit of truth, comes, He will guide you into all the truth. He will not speak on his own; He will speak only what He hears, and He will tell you what is yet to come.
> John 16: 13 (NIV)

Excitement, nervousness, relief and sadness; every emotion was going through us at the one time. This season was drawing to a close, for real now! No longer were we playing it out like a movie in our thoughts, we were actually standing on our launch pad.

Some days felt like nothing much was happening but then a day like today comes along when oceans of God sweep in like a flood to propel us further along. It was just what we needed and God knew it.

Whether you are experiencing a "Where are you God?" day, or a "Wow, God you really are here," revelation, the truth is, God has not moved away. His word is true. He is always, always, always, working and guiding us. He is the same God in the wow moments as He is in the silent ones. Keep trusting Him, keep under His glory cloud, He will turn up, loud.

MY GOD ALWAYS TURNS UP LOUD WHEN WE NEED IT

Day 65
STAYING UNDER THE GLORY CLOUD IS WORKING!

Staying under that glory cloud pays off. Just three days away from Paul checking into World Harvest Institute, we had an offer of a place to stay. Although Paul would be staying at the college for the first couple of weeks alone, which was funded from the released church funds, financially, we couldn't afford to stay there as a couple or with our kids. We had to find a place off site.

> And this same God who takes care of me will supply all your needs from his glorious riches, which have been given to us in Christ Jesus.
> Philippians 4:19 (NLT)

Their offer was amazing, a real bargain basement price! This host family told our mutual friend, who found the place for us that they usually charge fifty dollars per person per week and fifty dollars per person per week if they wanted to be fed. For some unknown incredible God reason, they agreed to the single's price of fifty dollars for our whole family to stay there. It was a very generous offer. We were so excited and accepted gratefully even though we didn't even have the fifty dollars per week at that point nor knew where it would come from but what we did know was, that somehow, just as God could bring forth water from a rock, He could also produce the resource we needed to pay our rent. It was very tempting to go that step further and agree to this family feeding us also, but we reasoned we could probably feed ourselves on even less than their incredible offer. Yes I know it sounds crazy, but we had lived on less over the past several years many times, so we were sure we could do it.

MY GOD SAYS, I WILL GO AND PREPARE A PLACE FOR YOU

Day 66 DON'T DOUBT THE GOD SOURCE

Today I began my career break from the bank. Having this part time bank job over the past several years was definitely a God given lifesaver. Not being full time meant we had to budget very tightly, yet God made every dollar stretch to do things we could not possibly do in the natural.

God given provision put back in His hands will surely multiply. That is what He does and that is why I am here telling you, "Don't doubt the source, the God source." You can trust Him with the little you have in your hands because that is all He needs to get you through and then some.

> Now that you know these things, you will be blessed if you do them.
> John 13:17 (NIV)

All we knew at this point in time was that we would go for one year and see what God unfolded. As I packed up my belongings for the last time, I stood at the door of the bank, turned around and thought to myself, "Will I ever return to this place again?"

We continued putting one step in front of the other every day. We began packing, preparing and targeting our departure date with confidence. James 2:22 kept working for us just as He promised. Our one step at a time motivated God to propel us ten more.

Excuse my repeating myself to you over and over but I feel I must! If nothing else touches you in this book, hold onto and practice this scripture because that is how God works. Works and faith, hand in hand, not one without the other and you must make the first move.

MY GOD IS A GOD WHO PROPELS US

Day 67   NOT ONE DAY TOO SOON

When we moved into our friend's house, they told us we could stay here until we left but the house would be on the market. We were not concerned about this because we had a sense in our spirit it would all work out. We had no idea just how worked out it would be.

We were one day out from Paul leaving to head to missions training and just two weeks until Belinda, Josh and myself would be joining him. Just two weeks before we were to close the doors behind us one last time. Just two more weeks!

> See, I am doing a new thing! Now it springs up; do you not perceive it? I am making a way in the wilderness and streams in the wasteland.
> Isaiah 43:29 (NIV)

Two weeks, and the significance of the two weeks this day became a landmark of confirmation of our timing when the owners of the house rang to tell us the house was not only sold, but the new owners would be moving in in two weeks time. Do you get it? Do you see it? We have an, on time, in time, never late God.

Proverbs 16:3 (NIV) says, "Commit to the Lord whatever you do and He will establish your plans." This is exactly what happened today, His plans were established deep within our hearts as this confirmation rang loud.

Other things were happening too. As time got closer to us leaving, the scurry of activity increased. Our church said they would put on a fundraiser dinner for us. They also confirmed their monthly support and friends poured finance into our hands regularly until the day we left. It was like the floodgates had opened. We had been chipping away for so long to see heaven open and now there was a downpour.

MY GOD IS A GOD WHO ESTABLISHES MY PLANS

Day 68 D DAY

Departure Day for Paul! The first of our family to sail into the sunset, well actually, he was catching a plane to Melbourne, his first stop before heading to Sydney for the start of training.

Coming home from the airport that day after dropping him off, I felt like we had moved from second gear straight to forth gear. The wheels were turning fast now and there was no time to think about how things would happen, we just needed to do, do whatever it took to be ready to board the Spirit of Tasmania, the ship that would take us to Melbourne on the 13th December.

As I walked in the door of the house a sudden weight of responsibility fell on me. It was now all up to me to make what was left to do happen. Paul needed to leave earlier to be on time for our training and it was a must for me to stay behind for our children to finish the school year.

I cried out to God, "Can I really do this alone?" And that still small voice that I had come to know so well reminded me that it was not Paul's strength I had been leaning on all this time but Gods and that He would not be leaving me to my own defenses just because Paul was not with us at this time. "I am your Alpha and Omega, your beginning and your end. I am with you. Keep leaning on me." It was reassuring that I could stand in His strength and what better place to stand.

Being just a one-hour flight from Tasmania to Melbourne, it was not long before Paul rang to say he had arrived safely at our mission agency. While sitting waiting to go into a meeting, he told me he had received a call from the pastor who had sparked the very first fire in our bellies for Vietnam during the missions summit in Hobart.

I will never forget the day that this pastor spoke of Vietnam and the plight of its people. Those words had hit us like a sword piercing the heart. It would not leave us and still today, eighteen years on,

> There is no longer Jew or Gentile, slave or free, male and female. For you are all one in Christ Jesus
> Galatians 3:28 (NLT)

Vietnam and its people continue to stir us to see them be all that God intends them to be, for them to live with purpose, hope and a future.

This particular pastor's phone call to Paul was brief yet significant. "Paul, remember I told you, those Vietnamese souvenirs and materials we gave you to sell, keep them, use the money to get to Vietnam. We don't require you to pay us back in any way, we believe in you."

When Paul told me this, I immediately reflected back on the email this pastor had sent, confirming the same thing. I have to admit I felt guilty at first knowing that the proceeds were orignally to go to the poor. I asked myself, is this right?

Time would soon tell, when we began to sell these products in some amazing and unusual ways. God was indeed keeping us from selling in the past to resource us for the future.

Lesson learnt. God is equally concerned about you and me, as He is with the rich or the underprivileged. Status does not matter to God, we matter to God.

MY GOD IS MY GALATIANS 3:28 AND HE IS YOURS TOO

Day 69 - 71 FLURRY OF ACTIVITY

As this chapter in our life was coming to a close, there were many last minute things to do. It can either overwhelm you or it can excite you as you continue to see the hand of God on everything. I chose the latter.

Amongst all God did over these few days, which were miraculous in themselves, what I desperately needed from God this week was for Him to bring to my remembrance everything I had learnt during my TESOL training in readiness for my final teaching presentation and assignments. Remember my humble beginnings, I didn't know which way was up when it came to English terminology. "Present Tense Continuous what?" This week's finals would either put a stamp of accreditation on me as a teacher, or I would have to go through it all again and there was no time for that. I needed that TESOL Certificate, the one vital piece of paper that was our golden ticket into Vietnam. Without it, we had no official purpose for going into the country.

My thoughts as I did my final preparation were, "Ok Deb, you've got this, but oh God, I hope you've got this God!"

As I sat down to begin my last assignment and lesson plan, I could sense God's presence in everything I wrote and in no time, it was done. I couldn't believe it. Holy Spirit done and dusted! A far cry from where I started.

> Keep your eyes open for God, watch for His works; be alert for signs of His presence. Remember the world of wonders He has made, His miracles, and the verdicts He's rendered.
> Psalm 105:4-5 (MSG)

Psalm 105:4-5 (MSG) Keep your eyes open for God, watch for His works; be alert for signs of His presence. Remember the world of wonders He has made, His miracles, and the verdicts He's rendered.

If James 2:22 is the key for action, Psalm 105:4-5 is the key to looking for God in all things, remembering who started it all back in Genesis and who's 'got this.'

MY GOD HAS ALWAYS 'GOT THIS'

Day 72 GET EDUCATED!

Today, another stake was put in the ground as Paul began his first day at mission training college. This environment saw Paul situated in a place of common minds and hearts to reach nations. Each one talking the same language, wanting to see lives changed, captives set free and the love of God spread far and wide. It was an inspiring atmosphere to be in before launching out into the wild.

Paul did the first three weeks of College without me. Lucky me, or maybe lucky him! They were full days, five days a week and full evenings too, if you were smart. Some students took it a bit easier through the week, relaxing in the evenings, but found themselves having to cram on the weekends to get all the assignments done and ready to hand in by Monday morning. I was proud of my husband, sticking to the plan we had worked on, to work our butts off during the week so we could have weekends to relax, be with family and enjoy church.

> Be equipped; be prepared, so the body of Christ can be built up.
> Ephesians 4:12 (NIV)

All too often over our years of being on the field have we seen many lone rangers come and go. They come to the field all exuberant, wanting to take on the world, but returned home disappointed simply from lack of preparation or training. Their hearts were always in the right place, but because they come without backing, without knowledge of the field and no training, when things didn't go to plan, they had nothing to fall back on.

Whatever God is calling you to, be prepared. Get trained, equipped, stay a learner. I can't say that enough. Learn, learn, learn. Keep moving forward, but learn along the way. It will be your saving grace. Never think you know it all or have it all together when you clearly know you don't. It is the wisest thing you can do. Humble yourself and learn. I still need to remind myself to do this.

MY GOD REQUIRES ME TO BE FULLY PREPARED

Day 73   I AM DONE!

High fiving myself today!

I handed in my assignments and did my practicum teaching. I can't believe I've made it. I am a transformed being, evolving from a once early school leaver, to a bonafide English Teacher. It was worth every struggle I overcame to achieve the intended goal and I even understand all those crazy terminologies now.

> You're blessed when you stay on course, walking steadily on the road revealed by God. You're blessed when you follow his directions, doing your best to find him. That's right - you don't go off on your own; you walk straight along the road he set. You, God, prescribed the right way to live; now you expect us to live it. Oh, that my steps might be steady, keeping to the course you set; Then I'd never have any regrets in comparing my life with your counsel. I thank you for speaking straight from your heart; I learn the pattern of your righteous ways. I'm going to do what you tell me to do; don't ever walk off and leave me.
> Psalm 119:108 (MSG)

At first, I didn't really want to do this course. I was just doing it because I needed to, so I sucked it up, and got on with it. Sometimes, to get to our destined future, we have to just do stuff whether we like it or not and we must approach it with a right attitude. It is only then we get the most out of it, remembering that nothing is wasted in God.

Learning, as I said before, is important and staying the course, finishing what you started, is vital. With the right heart and attitude, it will produce good fruit even though you may not love the whole process. Fruit such as patience, endurance, knowledge and the richness of meeting people in a field you hadn't encountered before. So let me encourage you, don't give up, what you gain from perseverance will carry you throughout life.

MY GOD REQUIRES US TO STAY THE COURSE

Day 74 BUT I NEED THIS FOR LATER!

Proverbs 3:5-6 tells us to trust in the Lord with all our heart and not to depend on our understanding, to seek His will in all we do and He will show us which path to take.

We had a bill to pay the following week and for a change, had the money in the bank for this one ahead of time. It was so nice to have it before it was due instead of just on time. Don't get me wrong, I was always totally grateful for all the 'just on times' God had had me believing for, but I have to admit, this ahead of time thing was more my style. I was feeling pretty relaxed about it and quite pleased with myself that we had this one covered. What I wasn't planning on though, was another bill coming in that would be due before the one I had been prepared for.

As usual, I cried out to God, as I had become very apt at doing, "God, we don't have the money for this one," and I had no sooner finished my not so holy prayer when God spoke ever so calmly to me saying, "Deb, you do have the money for it." "God, not the money for the Insurance bill? Remember, I planned in advance, it's wisely kept, I am a good steward girl!" And again God spoke, "I thought you trusted me in all things! Deb, all things are all things. Use what's in your hands."

All things are all things. You can't say to God, I trust you with my health, but I can't trust you with my work. Or I trust you with my finance, but I don't trust you with my kids. I know it is easier said than done, but we grieve God when we don't trust Him fully. Sometimes it is a day by day trust, even moment by moment, but trust we must. Whatever you need to trust God for today, tomorrow, next month, tell Him you trust Him and make a choice to do it, despite how you feel.

> For you are indeed God, and your words are truth; and you have promised me these good things.
> 2 Samuel 7:28 (LTB)

I chose trust. Trust in who God says He is, trustworthy. So in obedience to that trust, Paul and I used what was in our hands for that which we needed now, and rested in the knowledge He had the then sorted.

MY GOD IS FULLY TRUSTABLE

Day 75 WHAT GOD CAN DO IN JUST ONE HOUR

It was 8:30 in the morning and Belinda, Josh and I were just finishing breakfast when the phone rang. It was a friend of mine ringing to suggest I take all the Vietnamese products down to a trade show that was being held in a local church, down the road. She told me this fair would begin at 9:30am that morning and I should ring the organiser straight away. It sounded a good opportunity, but we were talking about a one hour turn around. I had one hour to ring the organiser, go across to the other side of the city where all our belongings were being stored, which was twenty minutes away, get to the trade fair that would take another twenty minutes, set up, and be ready to, hopefully sell. Calculating the whole scenario in my mind this exercise seemed impossible, but I thought, I have to try.

I rang the organiser straight away, but the phone rang out. There was no answer. I rang a second time and still no answer. I rang a third and forth time, and again, no answer. It was a further ten minutes before she picked up the phone and by then I was almost beside myself thinking, I have now ten minutes less to do this whole exercise. What seemed almost impossible before now seemed certainly that way. Now that I finally had this lady on the phone, I had to convince her I was not a strange invader, but someone who could be trusted as I explained who we were and what we were doing. She said, "OK I will agree if you can get here on time. There is only one small table in the corner left if you are happy with that." I said, "OK", hung up, rang the people looking after our gear, hoping they were home, which thankfully they were, grabbed my keys and bag and drove out the driveway and across to the other side of the city with under fifty minutes left on the clock. The traffic seemed busier than ever and time was ticking. I managed to get to our friends house in just over twenty minutes. We then had to find the boxes, among all our other boxes, (we had 65 in total), which took precious minutes to find. Then I had to not only get them into the car, but also fit them into the car, and then make my way to the fair. Inexplicably, I got to that church with five minutes to spare. I don't know how that happened. I grabbed just one of the boxes as all of them were big, and began running towards the entrance of the church hoping the organiser was at the front and she was. I introduced myself, and she led me to my table. I raced outside again to get the rest of those five large boxes and began setting up. By the time people started arriving, I was set up with a smile on my face but internally a whirlwind explosion of thoughts raced through my mind of what had taken place from one phone call just one hour before.

> So the sun stood still, and the moon stopped, till the nation avenged itself on its enemies, as it is written in the Book of Jashar. The sun stopped in the middle of the sky and delayed going down about a full day.
> Joshua 10:13 (NIV)

When I finally settled down on the inside, I scanned the room to see all the amazing and beautiful things that were for sale and knew that God would have to shine the light on my table if I were to sell anything. I had no doubt He would, because of the miraculous way He had got me here.

It wasn't just a light He shone. It was as if my table was illuminated as people came to my little stand in the corner and bought and bought and bought. I couldn't believe it. I had to chuckle inside at the wonder of God. Within the two and a half hour selling time slot, I sold $210 worth of stock. Doesn't sound much these days but in 1997, it was a lot.

I was an unknown among these people, who had no prior knowledge of me, but they had let me come at the last minute (literally) and not only allowed me to set up, but also charged no rent for the space. They also chose not to take a commission from my sales, which was usually the case.

That evening, we had some people come and visit us at home. They saw our boxes of stock and asked if they could have a look. They bought $90 worth of these anointed items. A total of $300 for the day! God of Wonder, above and beyond.

MY GOD IS A CLOCK STOPPER

Day 76 STOP TO PRAISE HIM

On this two hundred day miraculous deal I have going on with God, I have to say there has been a lot more get than give on my part. I have not been very reciprocal from my side so far, taking from my Master, my Lord, my Saviour, my Provider, each and every day, but, today I woke with a conviction upon me that I needed to stop and give back. It wasn't as if I didn't love Him, praise Him and worship Him, but I have to admit, most of the time I praised Him for what He was doing for me during these incredible days rather than who He is. Today was going to be different. It was time for me to stop and give to Him, my incredible daddy, God Almighty in all His deity, just because of who He is, and not for what He could do for me or for us, as a family.

It is so easy to get caught up in the I need and forget to just, "Be Still and Know that I am God." Psalm 46:10 (NIV)

> I shall run the way of Your commandments, For You will enlarge my heart.
> Psalm 119:32 (NASB)

For me, so far, I was discovering an amazing, resourceful, loving, faithful, promise filling God, and it was building my faith. I was growing so much through this journey, but it would be a very selfish relationship if it were just all about what He could do for me.

In my old journal that I am writing a lot of this from, on this day, I wrote, "Enlarge my borders of obedience to you." I love that. What if we prayed that prayer to God not just on one day but every day? Enlarge my borders of love for You, enlarge my borders of worship to You, enlarge my borders of time with You, sitting in Your presence, enlarge my borders of hearing You speak, gently and in power. What would happen? Who would we become? What would our relationship look like? A Garden of Eden experience, just enjoying His company for sure!

Stop, sit and be still in His presence and tell the Prince of Peace, the everlasting Father, you love Him and not ask of Him anything except to be closer to Him.

MY GOD WAITS FOR US TO SIT AT HIS FEET

Day 77
GOD DOESN'T TELL YOU EVERYTHING

I sat down to type up a prophecy we had received during this two hundred day journey and as I got towards the bottom of the page I realised, "Do no be afraid," appeared not just once, but was threaded throughout the whole second half of the word that had been given to us. There would be a statement, followed by the words, "Don't be afraid. You will go before leaders, but don't be afraid; you will see doors open where others haven't been, but don't be afraid; you will speak out boldly, but don't be afraid." These were amazing prophetic words, but we obviously needed to be reminded to not be afraid.

How many times did God give a command that would change a nation, a situation, a life; followed by saying, "Don't be afraid." It seemed there was a pattern to it all. It would begin with a big task, followed by challenging opposition, but resulting in victory.

What could we possibly be in for? At this point in time, all we knew was, we were to assist another couple who had begun a small work and teach English. I couldn't think of anything that would be so big, we would have to be reminded to not to be afraid. How could our behind the scenes, shuffling paperwork, doing administration for the leading couple and teaching a bit of English, warrant being afraid?

> Have I not commanded you? Be strong and courageous. Do not be afraid; do not be discouraged, for the LORD your God will be with you wherever you go."
> Joshua 1:9 (NIV)

You have to know, God will never give you the full picture of what is ahead. If He did, you would surely do a Moses and say, "Who am I? I think you have the wrong person. I couldn't possibly do that."

As I sit here many years later, I am glad God didn't tell us everything because as we began to forge forward in our place of ministry overseas, those words of not being afraid came in handy many times. What we had expected to come to do in Vietnam, turned out very differently, as often is the case.

Right here, can I say, keep your mind open to what things look like when you arrive at your destined place, be that on another field, or joining the Children's or music ministry or starting a new job. If you don't, you will feel confused and think you have missed it, but let me assure you, you not only have not missed it, but God has set it up. Yes, that's right, it has long been in His plan for you, but He needed to keep it from you for your own good. He actually wants to use you in a much larger way than you think you can do or achieve. He has more confidence in you, than you have in yourself. He knows the DNA within you and the unknown things that will unfold for you and He will cause those things to come to the surface as He works in and through you and the end result is, you will be amazed by what you are made of.

This is what we found when we finally stepped into our destiny in 1998. We were to go to Vietnam to assist another couple, but found they had to suddenly leave and we, their assistants, became assistants to ourselves leaving us with those words ringing in our hearts, "Do not be afraid." And that, my friend, is a whole other story.

MY GOD CALLS US TO BE UNAFRAID

Day 78 HISTORIC DAY

It was our last Sunday in church, the church we had come to serve in Tasmania. What a ride. Six years of laughing, crying and doing life with people who we grew to love for a lifetime. Today was my last opportunity to share with these wonderful people and leave a final deposit with them from the Word of God.

"Enlarge the borders of our tent," had been resonating within me all week. He had me enlarging the borders of giving back as I sat at His feet, but He was also showing me the importance of stretching in who we are.

If we are not continuing to enlarge who we are, we become stagnant. But there is no such thing as stagnant, because, if we are not moving forward, we begin to drift backwards. A river whose waters do not move become a quagmire. Things don't survive in a quagmire. We cannot assume we are OK just staying as we are. A quagmire grows slime on all that is caught within its borders. It becomes impossible to wade through and the waters are dark, murky and uninviting. A river is meant to be moving, running, clear, and refreshing, to keep alive all that swims beneath its surface. We can drink from a moving river and the fish that are birthed in its depths are good for eating.

> The Lord our God said to us at Horeb, "You have stayed long enough at this mountain."
> Deuteronomy 1:6 (NIV)

We are all called to extend our borders not only so we grow, but also so others can draw from what we have. It is the way we are made. Sharing that word this morning saw many people rededicate their lives to God afresh and vow to allow God to stretch them once again. It thrilled my heart to see so many hungry people promising to throw off restraints that had held them back and stepping into deeper waters to go beyond their stagnant state and fulfill God's purpose for their lives.

After the service, a trade table was set up for me to sell more wares from Vietnam and once again God blessed me with lots of sales. Ching Ching!

MY GOD DESIRES US TO BE A MOVING RIVER

Day 79   REMEMBER THE INSURANCE BILL?

You had to know that I had more than enough to pay that bill now from the incredible provision that was coming in through the Vietnamese products. On Wednesday, I could only see what was in my hand for this bill only, but God saw the abundance that was coming through the sale of previously unsaleable goods.

And of course, God is more than enough. Not only could we pay the insurance bill, but also several other accounts that were now due.

It is always worth listening to God. Sometimes we need to say to that self-voice inside our head, "Be silent. God is talking now!"

MY GOD IS AN ASTOUNDING PROVIDER

Day 80 STAYING HUMBLE

I cannot count the number of times over these past few months we found ourselves opening our front door to blessings. We would literally be on our way out, and friends or acquaintances would be arriving, each one coming with the same purpose, to bless us in some way. Take us shopping, give us money, give us a promise of long term support, help us pack or take us for dinner.

What you will find as you travel your own road, is that momentum will build and a gathering of people will begin to catch your vision and say, "We are behind you, we are on board." They may tell you, they can't go or do what you are going to do, but they can do something to help you get there.

> Humble yourself before the Lord (and with your friends and the fans you will gain), and He will lift you up in honour.
> James 4:10 (NLT)

For us, all the people who, now eighteen years ago, knocked on our door, are still championing our cause today. Why? Not only because they believed in what we were embarking on, but also because we put value on them for what they were doing for us. We wanted them to know that we would reciprocate to them, with genuine hearts, pray for their needs and stay connected.

It is important to note that no matter how much your, or our ministry grows, or how well known we become, humility must remain our default attitude. We should never get so big, either in what we do or in our influence that we think we no longer need those people who were part of our small beginnings because it was those people who helped us on our maiden voyage and who believed in us when we were struggling to believe in ourselves.

Stay humble in your journey, both when you are soaring on the mountaintops and working through your valleys. This is what God taught me today!

MY GOD REQUIRES ME TO SINCERELY VALUE ALL PEOPLE

Day 81 MY ABSOLUTE GOD

Proverbs 10:22 says, "Nothing we do, can improve on God." As I read the Word of God this morning, this verse leapt into my spirit with an overwhelming revelation of just how absolute and complete my God is. Wow, nothing can improve on Him. The word nothing is like the word all. Nothing means… nothing, just as the word all, means all.

Think about it for a moment, if we could just get our head around that, let it soak into our spirit, get a revelation of what this truly means, that His path, His way is complete and everything else is inferior, how much more would we lean into Him with a sigh of relief!

> God's blessings make life rich and nothing we do, can improve on God.
> Proverbs 10:22 (MSG)

With just four days, or four sleeps as children would say, remaining before we drove up to the top of the state to catch the boat, our biggest issue at hand today was figuring out how on earth were we going to move all our furniture and belongings which we still possessed (and had not been sold in the garage sale) into storage at our friend's house. I knew my faithful Subaru just wasn't going to cut it. No one I knew of owned a truck and hiring one for so few items would not only be a waste, but expensive. What have you got in mind God?

I have no idea how a pastor we hardly knew from the south of the state heard about our need but before the day was out, he was on the phone to me offering to move our gear in his truck and to just name to date and time! How can you improve on that?

MY GOD CAN DO ANYTHING YOU KNOW!

Day 82 MY GREEN RUG

I know it sounds silly but I was very precious about my green rug. I could have sold it many times over during our garage sale days and although we needed the money, it held too many precious memories for our family. Over the past six years, that rug heard stories told to our children as we sat on it. It shared Bible studies with our cell group each and every week. It caught the spill of the many meals eaten on it and besides all this, it was just a very nice rug. If I could have taken it to Vietnam, I would have, but it was way too big for that.

A close friend of mine knew how much this rug meant to me so offered to use it in her own home as if it were her own. To me, it was the second best thing to having it in my own place because I knew she would love it like I did. I was also happy not to be putting it in yet another box.

My friend Gayle knew me so well and we did a lot together during our Tasmanian season. Our kids played together, we socialised as a family often and she would walk the streets of Hobart with me to try and drum up trade for our failing business. I couldn't think of a better person to share my prized possession with. Today she came by to pick it up and I was able to say farewell to it, knowing it was in good hands.

> Indeed, the very hairs of your head are all numbered. Don't be afraid (to ask); you are worth more than many sparrows.
> Luke 12:7 (NIV)

There were other things that were being looked after during this first year we were to spend overseas, things that weren't quite so precious as my green rug but were worth keeping and we were grateful for friends who offered to take care of them for us.

God is not just concerned about all the big things that mean so much to us, but also all the little things that are often just as important to us. Don't be afraid to ask Him to look after those little things that matter to you and your family. He is all about the all.

MY GOD UNDERSTANDS AND TAKES CARE OF THE THINGS THAT MATTER TO US

Day 83 CAN IT BE?

I can't believe this is the last night we will spend in Tasmania. In some ways, the time has flown and in other ways it seems we have been here forever. Packing our car today made it all so final. We truly were leaving.

It took all day to get everything out of the house, transported to storage, pack what we were taking into the car and clean what had been our home for the past few months. Many came to help us pack and move while others came to give us money and even buy more of our Vietnamese products. The overwhelming support was incredible and made us feel so loved.

At midnight we forced the last bag into the remaining sliver of space in our Subaru before climbing into bed on this our very last night. It felt good knowing everything was finally done yet incredibly surreal as finality came closing in on this chapter of our lives. My final thought as I drifted off to sleep was gratefulness. Gratefulness for both the faithfulness of God and for the love of all those helping hands!

MY GOD DELIGHTS IN THE BODY OF CHRIST WORKING TOGETHER

Day 84 HERE WE GO!

Today is the 13th December 1997. I hadn't really thought much of our departure date except that it worked out for us to leave on this day but I suddenly realised that six years earlier, the 13th December 1991 was the day we arrived in Tasmania. It wasn't planned that way but here we were leaving on a date that began and finished a season. We arrived in Tasmania to a word that was hard to chew on, "Hard times ahead" (that lovely prophetic word), and we were leaving on a more promising word, that He gave us out of Isaiah 40:2, "Your hard task is now completed," (NIV) says, "Speak tenderly to Jerusalem, and proclaim to her that her hard service has been completed."

I don't believe it was by accident that we were leaving on such an appointed day. God seems to do things like this for us, just as He had done by providing the house we had been living in rent free for the exact time needed before the new owners were coming in.

Our trip to Devonport, where the Spirit of Tasmania docked, was an easy one and quite uneventful. We arrived to see the lines of cars waiting to board, cars carrying families going on holidays or moving states, and others going on business trips by sea rather than air. Many were like us, packed to the brim with their worldly possessions. We pulled up behind the last car and in no time many other cars were lined up behind us. We needed to stretch our legs after an almost four hour trip and as I walked to the back of the car, a young man in the car directly behind us quickly jumped out of his car bounding straight up to me. I thought, is this someone I am supposed to know? I am pretty good at remembering faces but I didn't recognise him at all. He was so excited as he approached me and he couldn't wait to ask me what was obviously bubbling up inside him when he noticed us pull up. I was surprised by what came out of his mouth. "Are you going overseas to teach English?" "Um, yes I am." I had hardly answered him when he replied, "I am too, I saw your TESOL book and Bible and thought, you must be! I am going to China." Talk about a God moment. He was going to be right next-door, country wise. He then asked me, "Where are you heading now?" I told him that we were heading to Sydney to pick up my husband and then travelling to our hometown of Newcastle for Christmas. If his eyes could have popped out, I think they would have. "I am heading there too, my hometown is Newcastle also." If there was any niggling doubt in me as we were about to take our final step off the island of Tasmania, this little divine appointment dispelled it. There was no need for any more uncertainty, God you are amazing!

> Let your eyes look directly forward, and your gaze be straight before you. Ponder the path of your feet; then all your ways will be sure.
> Proverbs 4:25-26 (ESV)

Within an hour, everyone was on board and heading up to the main deck. After finding out where our cabin was situated, Belinda, Josh and I went straight there. It was an overnight journey, which was a nice relaxing way to unwind after the whirlwind week we had just experienced.

As I lay in my bed that night I looked through the porthole and realised, this porthole is facing in the direction of where we are going, not where we had been. God was reminding me once again, that it truly was He, who was leading us out.

It is so important for us to look forward and be focused on what lies ahead, to be fully engaged and embrace the next season. We cannot have one hand on the past and one on the future if we truly want to succeed and be fulfilled.

MY GOD IS A GOD WHO WANTS US LOOKING FORWARD

Day 85 – 91 TAKING IT SLOW TO SYDNEY

We arrived at the dock in Melbourne on the dot of 5.00am. I had never driven in Melbourne before and was feeling a bit apprehensive. There was no such thing as Google maps back then to tell you to turn right here, left there and whoops, you just made a wrong turn so adjust at the next available street. No this was the days of hard book maps and instinct. I was so proud of myself as I didn't get lost once, which is a huge victory for me. Anyone who knows me well knows I am hopeless with directions. Paul will tell you and he teases me about it often.

> The Lord says, "I will teach you the way you should go; I will instruct you and advise you."
> Psalm 32:8 (GNT)

It was Sunday and we couldn't wait to get to our friend's house there in Melbourne in time to go to church with her. It was going to be so refreshing soaking in church without having to do anything.

I was glad we had decided to take this trip slowly so we could relax with friends and family in Melbourne and Canberra before taking on the Sydney traffic. We also visited our Mission Centre to have our last briefing and it was nice to be encouraged for what we were about to embark upon.

Travelling the Hume Highway was a bit daunting for me, but I had to stay strong and confident so our kids would not feel unsafe. I told myself the car had just been serviced so it shouldn't break down and I knew if I just followed the road signs I would get there.

Sydney streets were like a maze but I knew God was with me as He helped me navigate every turn until we drove into the college where we were greeted by the best sight we had seen in two weeks – Paul, who was waiting with open arms. Finally, we were together again.

As pleased as I was with myself, getting safely to Sydney, it was nice to hand over the driving reins to Paul again. We made our way up to Newcastle, to enjoy Christmas with extended family.

**MY GOD IS MY NAVIGATOR
ON THE STREETS AND IN MY LIFE**

Day 92 THE LIVING WORD, OUR LIVING WORD

I just loved how God's Word was growing strong inside me. This journey of pressing in to Him daily, seeking His face, looking to see how He would appear in each and every day made me feel like I was touching heaven. Some days were challenging and there were times I lacked faith but as God turned up without fail, I got to know the depth of His love and desire to be so intimately connected to me and what He was drawing us into as a family. I was learning His language of love and His power through the living Word.

This morning I woke to these two scriptures resounding in my very being. They were messages from heaven.

- Be strong and of good courage, fear not, nor be afraid of them, for the Lord thy God, He it is that does go with you, He will not fail you, or forsake you. Deuteronomy 31:6 (NKJV)
- There has never been the slightest doubt in my mind that the God who started this great work in you would keep at it, and bring it to a flourishing finish on the very day Christ Jesus appears. Philippians 1:6 (MSG)

It was Sunday and it felt so good to be back in our old home church again seeing so many familiar faces. After the service, our senior pastor called us to the front so the church could pray for us, and as he did, the prophetic word flowed for each of us.

> For we do not have a high priest who is unable to empathize with our weaknesses, but we have one who has been tempted in every way, just as we are--yet he did not sin. Hebrew 4:15 (NIV)

I would love to say mine said, oh you amazing woman of valor, of great strength, courage and faith but it didn't. The word for me was don't worry, be confident, don't be anxious, God will provide. I was definitely growing in my relationship with God but if I said, it was perfect now and I had it all together, that would be a lie. I still struggled in my human weakness some days more than others. Paul says in Romans 7:15-20, "I do what I don't want to do, and don't do what I should do," which has always been a great comfort to me. If Paul, a great example for us, struggled, and God still used him, He can use me and He can still use you. We just have to be honest with God and say, "Sorry God, I blew it," but get up again and keep putting that one foot in front of the other with a YES Lord mentality.

Paul, Belinda and Josh also received words that confirmed our calling which was so encouraging for our kids in particular to receive, because this call was not just one Paul and I were following, but it was one God was calling us to as a family.

A beautiful start to our Christmas break.

MY GOD IS A GOD WHO CAN WORK WITH OUR STRUGGLES

Day 93 – 99 GOD HAS GOT FAMILY COVERED

We had been so focused on ministry and all that had to be done for so long, it was nice to stop for a while and soak in time with family, especially my beautiful, Godly grandmother.

If it weren't for my grandmother, I wouldn't be who I am today. My beautiful grandmother loved everyone unconditionally. My grandmother, the intercessor! Every morning she would get up and before doing anything else, bend her knees before her Lord to pray for nations, governments, missionaries who served God all around the world and of course, pray for each and every family member. She would give generously, without hesitation, from her small government pension, and still had more than enough as God blessed her giving. Her love for God was undeniable and unshakeable.

We have a great family, and without a doubt they love us completely, but it was very difficult for them to fully grasp why we would 'leave' them. As we sat around the dinner table enjoying one of the last meals we would have together for a while, one by one they began letting us know just how unhappy they were with our decision and that it just wasn't right. Immediately I felt heartsick. We didn't know what to say. To know they didn't approve made it one of the hardest challenges we had faced so far in our journey. This was not a decision we had taken lightly, but through a lot of soul searching, weighing up the sacrifice and trusting God to take care of the family we would leave behind. We had to follow God's leading for us as a family, continue to say YES to God, trusting the Holy Spirit to minister to them, to be ok and at peace with the decision in time, and we needed to love them through it.

The greatest challenge you will find when you make the decision to move forward with your life as God directs you often comes from those closest to you. It is not that they don't love you, care for you or want the best for you, but when it effects them personally, they may question the decision you made, is in fact from God. This is why I say repeatedly; the decisions you make need to be a God thing, not just a good thing.

Good things are great, they could even work out but when things get tough, questioning comes, doubt is put in your mind by others or even yourself, and you can crumble. But when it is a God thing, that deep knowing conviction in your spirit is an anchor for your soul and when you are standing in that position, you will not yield.

Now that I was on leave from the bank, we had no finance at all to draw from which meant each day's provision needed to fall like manna from heaven.

Of course we prayed but were surprised how God answered. Not through outsiders, supporters or churches but through our family. We had not asked them for anything nor did we walk around in sackcloth and ashes to give them or anyone else a hint that we needed help, but God had whispered in their ear and they responded. Our hearts were moved as our precious family gave us food, finance, paid bills and even lent us a mobile phone. Already God was working a miracle in their hearts.

In saying all that, I want to say this, ministry is important, purpose and plans of God are important, stay the course, but family is family. Savour your family. You may be living close or far, the distance doesn't matter, just make the time to write, ring or text them to let them know you love them. That is all it takes.

> When all the people were safely across, the Lord said to Joshua, "Tell the twelve men chosen for a special task, one from each tribe, each to take a stone from where the priests are standing in the middle of the Jordan, and to carry them out and pile them up as a monument at the place where you camp tonight." So Joshua summoned the twelve men and told them, "Go out into the middle of the Jordan where the Ark is. Each of you is to carry out a stone on your shoulder — twelve stones in all, one for each of the twelve tribes. We will use them to build a monument so that in the future, when your children (those close to you) ask, 'What is this monument for?'" Joshua 4:1-6 (TLB)

You may wonder how this scripture relates but when I read it, I believe God was saying that He sends us to do His work, to create something lasting and one day, those close to us (who didn't understand in the beginning) will one day say, "Tell us what you are doing for the Lord."

MY GOD HAS GOT THOSE CLOSE TO YOU, CLOSE TO HIM

Day 100
WORLD HARVEST INSTITUTE AND ALL THAT FOOD!

It was hard saying goodbye to our kids last night, needing to leave them behind in Newcastle with friends so we could commence (recommence for Paul) our mission training in Sydney. Because our budget (or more precisely, non-budget) didn't allow for us to have them with us, we had to make the difficult decision of doing this part of the journey without them by our side. Being the first time we had left Belinda and Josh for an extended period of time, this six week study block and a one hundred and sixty kilometre distance between us, emotionally stretched us all. Although our intention was to drive up and see them at weekends, we knew this would only be possible when God provided the petrol to get us there. This meant we had to believe God was not only the God of our resource to get us to our beloved new country, but that He was also the same faithful God who would protect and care for our kids in our absence.

Day one of World Harvest Institute for me was intense. With the all day lectures, mountains of reading and assignments that followed, my head was in a spin. It was not like my TESOL course where I could digest one mouthful at a time concentrating on just one subject. Here there were several major subjects to learn and write about one after the other. Five hours of lectures followed by three articles to read, interact with and report on which took a further three hours and then for dessert, learn a new language. Yeah, no problem! I now understood why Paul wasn't ringing me too often during those first three weeks when he was here on his own. There was just no time!

Morning tea, afternoon tea and lunch were welcomed sanity stops. I couldn't believe the great food that was on offer for morning and afternoon tea, and it was free. Just what we needed! We had very little resources left from what was given to us over Christmas so we ate as much as we could to fill our stomachs, hoping we didn't look like gluttons in the process. By doing this we could skimp on our lunch bill, which we intended to buy off campus. Being my first day at college though, we really wanted to bond with the other students so we made the decision to stay around for lunch. This meant we had to buy from the college campus diner, but building relationships with our fellow students was more important to us than being concerned about the money. These were the people we would be doing life with over the coming month and a half so it was an investment rather than a cost.

> For He satisfies the thirsty and fills the hungry
> with good things.
> Psalm 107:9 (NIV)

It was definitely money well spent as we sat listening to these students tell of their own amazing stories on how God provided and opened doors on their behalf to get them to this point. Hearing about their heart for the nation they were called to with the same enthusiasm and passion that was in our own hearts for Vietnam, said we were in good company. Today, eighteen years on, we have managed to stay connected with some of these amazing people and hear about both their victories and challenges.

MY GOD, WHO FEEDS BODY AND SOUL

Day 101 – 104
DISCIPLINE AND CRAZY PAYS OFF

It was always a great feeling to arrive at lectures each morning and before sitting down, proudly go to the designated tray marked 'Assignment Work in Here' to place our completed previous day's given task work. Many times that tray was light on as some had chosen to relax in the evenings and cram at weekends. It was very tempting for us to do the same because the last thing we felt like doing was more study and writing after a full day of doing just that, but were motivated to keep going by thoughts of our kids. Every weekend possible, we were going to spend with our kids.

Money was getting low now and payment for board was looming. It was a crazy idea, but we decided to go check our bank just to see if fifty dollars had magically appeared from nowhere for our rent. We were not expecting any payments from the Government, as they informed us so clearly when we asked. Nor were we expecting any support from our ministry partners before going to the field, but we checked anyway. I remember it clearly as if it were yesterday, I nervously stood behind Paul as he put in our card to check our balance. I wanted to look but I couldn't, so I chose to stare at the scenery around us. Paul pinned in the appropriate numbers, got the balance, retrieved the card, took the receipt and turned to me with his usual 'poker' face as he handed me that white slip of paper. I quickly glanced down at it and saw numbers. Positive ones. I couldn't believe it. There was money there and it came from the government. "But they said we couldn't get anything even for the kids." We were so excited but thought we had better check with our government agency to make sure it was correct and they hadn't given it to us by mistake. After a quick phone call, they confirmed that yes, we were entitled to get family payments for our children. It wasn't a huge sum but it was enough. Enough to pay our board, to feed ourselves another day, and buy that all important petrol

> For the moment all discipline seems painful rather than pleasant, but later it yields the peaceful fruit of righteousness to those who have been trained by it.
> Hebrews 12:11 ESV

to go see our kids!

It was a great feeling to drive down the highway at the end of that first week knowing we were only hours away from giving our kids the biggest hugs ever. There was no Skype, FaceTime, Facebook or reliable Internet back then, just your regular phone that charged high rates because Sydney to Newcastle was classed as a long distant phone call and that meant we could only ring for a couple of minutes on a few occasions. To finally see Belinda and Josh's beautiful faces made pushing ourselves hard to get those last assignments in for the week one hundred percent worthwhile.

MY GOD HONOURS THOSE WHO HAVE DISCIPLINED DETERMINATION

Day 105 - 106 ONE DAY AT A TIME!

After a nice relaxing Saturday, it was again a great privilege to have another opportunity to share our vision for Vietnam in church. The pastors of this church were long standing friends of ours so we didn't need to convince them we were a good investment. In fact, they had already indicated beforehand that they would support us, so the pressure was off, and knowing they had a guest speaker, our only job was to do our ten minute 'vision catching' spiel!

When we arrived at the church we learnt that the invited pastor was well known for moving in the prophetic and I just knew in my spirit before he even got up to utter a word, that he would call us out, and call us out he did. What he spoke over us could have come right out of the pages of this journal, that our walk was a day by day journey.

> "I have a great sense that in the days that lie ahead the Lord would keep you in a place where you don't become relaxed in the things that you are doing (oh really, I never would have guessed), but keep in an attitude of total commitment day by day and as you keep walking in that place of commitment He will continue to

direct your footsteps day by day. I sense it's a real living thing, you living day by day as the Lord directs you."

The 'day by day this and day by day that', kept announcing it's way throughout the prophetic word. It wasn't new news to us, this day by day thing. We had been walking it since back in September when I (because it was I that needed it. Paul, the unshakable faith man, didn't need it) had got on my knees and asked God to give us something each day until we left our Aussie shores. Today was just a confirmation that we were right in the centre of God's perfect will for this moment in time. However, it did refuel our confidence in this process and had not grown stale in God's mind, but in fact proved to us that even that September prayer was actually orchestrated by God Himself for the purpose of helping us to see Him in our every day.

> The steps of good men are directed by the Lord. He delights in each step they take.
> Psalm 37:23 (TLB)

The weekend had gone by so fast and again, we had to say goodbye to our kids, but that confirming word gave us strength to keep going, knowing every step we took brought us closer to completing our studies, being reunited with our kids and heading off to our promised land.

**MY GOD IS A GOD WHO ORDERS OUR STEPS,
ONE DAY AT A TIME**

Day 107 MAKING LECTURE TIME FUN

As hard as it was to say goodbye to our kids, it was nice to again be with such like-minded people.

Class times were strict, but I understood why. We had so much to consume in such a short amount of time. Being in a school type environment, with bells to tell you school was in, and lecturers letting us know in no uncertain terms we had to be on time, I found myself watching the clock closely, dare I be put on detention! Of course, they were not hard taskmasters. They simply took their ministry seriously and both Paul and I appreciated that they had our best interests at heart, wanting us to gain the most from their own personal life's work and testimonies.

This week lectures, reading and assignment work still took eight hours every day, but I was getting the hang of it now. I do admit, some of the lectures were extremely fascinating and I particularly enjoyed hearing the lecturer's personal stories that brought everything we were learning about to life.

We also had our lighthearted moments in class. In fact we had our very own in-house soap opera, we shall call "The love you, love you not drama, of two students." It was something to look forward to every day as a mental break from the intensity of lectures. You couldn't wait for the next episode. These two lovebirds would sit together chatting and smiling at each other one day only to not even give each other a second glance the next. Then there were the times they would call each other girlfriend and boyfriend only to have one party deny it by end of the day after yet another argument. The talk of marriage even came up at one point only to be dispelled following one more disagreement between them, and that idea was soon put to bed when the girlfriend stated, for the record, that there would be no marriage happening here. And so are the days…

> It is possible to give away and become richer! It is also possible to hold on too tightly and lose everything. Yes, the liberal man shall be rich! By watering others, he waters himself.
> Proverbs 11:25 (TLB)

And just how did we know all this was happening? Let's just say it wasn't a silent film. We couldn't predict how that story would end, but we were pretty sure it would not be well.

Morning tea was something else we looked forward to during the day for obvious reasons. We needed the food (LOL), but we also loved using this time to get to know our fellow students. On this occasion, as we walked out of the building and headed towards the glorious array of food that was waiting to be consumed, one of the students came up behind us, and whispered discretely to us, "God has spoken to me and to told me to give you this." She put an envelope in our hands and said God bless you. We knew it had to be money and as we took the envelope from her hand we said 'thank you.' We felt completely humbled by such an unexpected gift from this fellow student, who was also believing God for her daily bread, just like everyone else there was, yet out of her obedience to God, she chose to give. She was saying 'YES' to God, a great test of faith and obedience on her part and no doubt God would bless her in return! I opened the envelope and took out the bright yellow note, a fifty dollar note. The exact amount we needed for our board. How was she to know, except through God!

**MY GOD BRINGS RESOURCE TO NEED
WHERE YOU WOULD NOT DARE TO LOOK**

Day 108   99C LASAGNAS

In our quest for cheap meals, Paul and I had discovered 99 cent lasagnas at a local supermarket. These little gems became our daily staple as they managed to fill our stomachs and match our budget. We would share one at lunchtime and take one home for dinner. We were a little embarrassed about eating our 99c lasagna in front of our hosts so we always waited until they were well and truly finished with their own dinner and away from the dining table before we would go heat up our humble meal.

Often we would come home to their table laid out and dressed with their evening meal. What would it be tonight? Roast dinner, Italian spaghetti, sausages and vegetables or a hearty soup? Whatever they were serving up, it always smelled divine. Our stomachs would ache, as our taste buds went into overdrive, screaming with desire for what they were having. Sometimes they would ask if we would like to dine with them, but we always declined, saying we had our own meal sorted and thanked them before escaping to our bedroom. We could not afford a further one hundred dollars per week for this family to feed us, so we used the time they ate to dive into our readings for the evening. After they had well and truly finished their dinner, we would take a break to 'feast' on our own special meal.

> Go, eat your food with gladness, and drink your wine with a joyful heart, for God has already approved what you do.
> Ecclesiastes 9:7 (NIV)

As we arrived home this night though, things were to be different. We walked through the front door with lasagna in hand as usual, and headed towards our bedroom. We'd hardly reached the doorway when we were called to the kitchen. "We would like to invite you for dinner." We assumed they meant the usual, 'we can feed you if you like', so again, we thanked them and said we were OK, that we had something for dinner. But tonight, they weren't buying our 'we are ok' story. "Paul and Deb, we are not asking you join us as boarders, but as our guests, no money. You can save your lasagna for another night."

I wanted to cry. We had tried so hard to hide our little secret, but somehow they just knew. We thanked them profusely and for the first time, sat with our host family to enjoy the best meal we had had since arriving in Sydney, and this night was to become the first of many nights they would set a place for Paul and I, inviting us to join them.
Thank you God.

MY GOD IS A GOD WHO SAYS "YOU KEPT YOUR ATTITUDE SWEET WHEN ALL YOU HAD WERE 99 CENT LASAGNAS, SO NOW I WILL REWARD YOU WITH BANQUETS"

Day 109 - 111 ATTITUDE IS EVERYTHING

From that day on, we not only received free meals each day from our hosts, but they also welcomed our kids to stay with us free.

Attitude is everything. It comes back to the glass half full, or glass half empty perspective. We could have complained about the fact we were the only ones who had to survive on 99 cent meals each day. We could have complained that we only got to see our family occasionally. We could have complained that while others went to the movies, ate out at restaurants and bought things, we had to go straight home, and lock ourselves behind closed doors with our small meal. We could have complained about others getting benefits to help them get through college while we were not accepted for any allowance at all. But thank God, we chose the glass half full attitude, and praised Him for feeling full on our mini meals, for providing morning and afternoon tea free, and giving us a comfortable bed to sleep in each night. Thank God we stayed grateful to Him for willing friends who took care of our beautiful kids one hundred and sixty kilometres away so we could complete our studies and that He continued to surprise us with provision in all sorts of ways. He turned up every day on this journey, paving the road each step of the way.

Attitude will make or break you, but others also notice how you react or respond to situations in your life. It's not just God who takes note of it, but those around you also. I believe keeping our attitude sweet was one of the reasons why our host family began to include us in their family life.

> Be glad you can do the things you should be doing.
> Do all things without arguing and talking about how
> you wish you did not have to do them.
> Philippians 2:14 (NLV)
>
> Look through me, O God, and know my heart. Try
> me and know my thoughts. See if there is any sinful
> way in me and lead me in the way that lasts forever.
> Psalm 139:23-24 (NLV)

MY GOD IS A GOD WHO TESTS OUR HEART

Day 112 – 116
THE CALL, THE VISION BUT NO CONCRETE EVIDENCE

As I have said so many times already, this path we travel will never be one hundred percent black and white, clear as crystal, with all our ducks lined up in a row. No, that is neither reality, nor faith driven. When we can't see everything coming together in the natural, we have to stay fixed on the knowledge that God is standing in the gap, in the centre of it all, putting unseen things in place.

In the centre of any building there is a weight bearing beam that holds everything in place, while all the surrounding parts come together to create the structure that was in the mind of the creator before construction began. While it is being built, it's easy to look at it and think, "Not much work has been done on this building lately." But without you realising it, electricians have been wiring, plumbers have been putting drainage in and builders have been shoring up the foundations. Looking from the outside, there may seem to be so many parts that are not even in place and you wonder, will this actually be ready for opening day?

As we entered our sixth week of World Harvest Institute, we still had no definite confirmation, or concrete evidence, that showed we could actually get into the country we knew we were called to. God had confirmed it to us by His Spirit, His Word and prophesy telling us to prepare and keep moving forward, that He would do what we could not do, but in the natural things didn't seem to be moving along that quickly and it was tempting to point out to God, that not much work had been done on our building lately.

We'd had the call for years, but this final 200-day faith walk, that began back in September the year before, was now into its 116th day and up until this day we were still waiting to hear if we would even be accepted by the government of Vietnam to enter the country.

It was so easy to get despondent and anxious, wondering if God had gone on holiday for a while because nothing seemed to be happening. We would look at the structure and only see the holes. It was in those times we realised we had moved our focus off the Master Builder and onto our own ability. It wasn't until we refocused our attention to the One who called us, that our world became clear again, and we saw standing in the middle of our construction site, the Master Weight Bearer, holding everything together and confidently saying, "I've still got this."

> The fundamental fact of existence is that this trust in God, this faith, is the firm foundation under everything that makes life worth living. It's our handle on what we can't see. The act of faith is what distinguished our ancestors, set them above the crowd.
> Hebrews 11:1-2 (MSG)

It is always nice however, when we did see another wall go up, bringing shape to the finished product. On day 116, we finally got news to say that the Vietnamese Government was looking favorably on us coming in. Although this was more of a toilet wall sized confirmation rather than a living-room wall, it was still a wall, and we knew it was definitely God putting those pieces into place.

Don't ever think God has taken a break. He has never let go of the weight-bearing centre of your construction and He directs from that position. Stay focused on Him, He is still building even if you cannot see it clearly during the process.

MY GOD WHO HOLDS THE CENTRE OF MY WORLD REMINDS ME HE'S STILL GOT THIS

Day 117 ALWAYS COVERED

I didn't know what to write about today because no great revelation had come to me on this one. I asked the Holy Spirit, what I could say about these fourteen words scribbled in my journal on the 15th January 1998. Come on Holy Spirit say something! Immediately He spoke, "Deb, read between the lines you have written."

My scribble consisted of "WHI continues, $430 went into bank, this covers board, last of WHI fees, Insurance, etc." As I re-read those few seemingly unimportant words, the Holy Spirit spoke, "You know Deb, every day, I have you covered. I have it all covered. I work continually on your behalf behind the scenes so that you can declare that I am faithful." That was enough, words spoken directly from Almighty God Himself, telling me, He had it covered. He had it covered then and He still has it covered today.

We have no idea the lengths and breadths God goes to in order to come through for us every day. May we not be flippant in our gratitude as we read between the lines of what He is doing for us.

That is for someone out there reading this now. Trust Him, He has got all your needs covered!

MY GOD NEVER LEAVES US NOR FORSAKES US

Day 118 LANDMARK DAY

It's Friday 16th January 1998. One year ago today, we went to Vietnam for the first time as a family. As I write this, I can't help but be thrust back to that day like it was yesterday. Dream became reality on that day as we embarked on that first journey that would become the first step for a lifetime. Little did we know that that visit would shake us to our core for this nation, and still does today, eighteen years on.

Landmarks are important. They are concrete markers to gauge how you are tracking. In your pursuit towards your goals, your destiny, your purpose, take time to celebrate the landmarks, how far you have come rather than how much further you need to go. This is important, as it will spur you on to keep on going forward. Even when you are just starting out, celebrate the fact that you actually did start out, rather than staying in that safe seat of mundaneness. Celebrate the fact that in your starting out, you are in the minority of those who say, I am going to put my stamp on this earth, to make a difference and fulfill the plans God intended for me to do.

Keep your eyes on God when the road gets hard. Even if you find yourself walking on water, passing through the Red Sea or possibly in the den of lions, remember, He has not left you. God is walking on the water with you! He is holding your hand as you pass through the Red Sea and surrounding you in that den of lions. He is with you all the way, refining, building, strengthening you and continuing to catapult you forward as you stay on the path. When you come through those times, you will look back and see just how strong you are becoming, readying yourself for greater things ahead and at that point, you establish another landmark.

Landmarks have got me through when things have not gone the way I expected and even questioned why things had to be that way only to realise, God was building resilience inside of me for greater things. Embrace the good and the difficult road to your destiny, as it will only make you stronger.

> When you go through deep waters and great trouble, I will be with you. When you go through rivers of difficulty, you will not drown! When you walk through the fire of oppression, you will not be burned up—the flames will not consume you. For I am the Lord your God, your Savior, the Holy One of Israel.
> Isaiah 43:2-4 (TLB)

MY GOD HELPS ME NAVIGATE THE HARD ROADS

Day 119 - 120   A TASTE OF VIETNAM

I absolutely love the fact that Australia is so multicultural. One of my favourite places in Australia is Melbourne, not because of the weather, but its diverse cultures and people. If you want to eat a dish from anywhere in the world, you are bound to find it in a restaurant owned by people from that country in Melbourne. Sydney also has much culture and just up the road from our college was a Vietnamese community. When we arrived in Bankstown, it was like walking into little Vietnam. The shops and restaurants were dressed in true Vietnamese style and Vietnamese signage was prominent throughout the streets. As we walked through those streets, the familiar smells of lemongrass and coriander wafted up our nostrils and we couldn't help but dive into the nearest restaurant to take in that fabulous aroma. We felt so at home!

"Felt so at home." A great indicator of God preparing our hearts to immerse ourselves into what would become our future home, a land to possess.

When sands shift in your life, you will find home takes on a whole new perspective. Home may become a different country like Vietnam is for us, or it could be shifting from one ministry to another, or one field of work to a completely different one, but you will know what is home for you when it feels right and the home of the past no longer does.

> For the land, into which you are entering to possess it, is not like the land of Egypt from which you came, where you used to sow your seed and water it with your foot like a vegetable garden. But the land into which you are about to cross to possess it, a land of hills and valleys, drinks water from the rain of heaven, a land for which the Lord your God cares; the eyes of the Lord your God are always on it, from the beginning even to the end of the year.
> Deuteronomy 11:10-12 (NASB)

MY GOD IS A GOD WHO PREPARES HEARTS FOR NEW PLACES

Day 121 – 127 BE AWARE

When we're embarking on a new season, one that involves stepping into what God is purposing for us, the enemy will pull out all stops to try to bring discouragement, distraction, disunity or disappointments to get us to the point of saying, "It's just too hard."

Documenting your journey is important. No, I would say vital, because it reminds you that no matter how you may feel, what the circumstances may say or the opposition you may receive from others, re-reading your journal entries will encourage you once again. Looking over all the struggles you came through and the victories you have won up until this point, will once again spur you on. What you will read between the lines is just how much God believes in you and that He has indeed chosen you for this very purpose, and with that in mind, you can remind the devil, "With God on my side, nothing is impossible."

As we began yet another week of college I had to give myself this same self-talk. I found myself listening to the wrong voice in my moment of weakness. "Look at how far you have to go. How are you going to pay your rent this coming week? Do you really think you are going to get all the support you need? You're not smart enough to even graduate this class."

Yes, the devil plays dirty. He will hit places that are tender. I didn't do well at school due to family circumstances, only managing to just scrape through to gain my year ten certificate, leaving school just before my sixteenth birthday. I never went on to the higher

> The tongue can bring death or life; those who love to talk will reap the consequences.
> Proverbs 18:21 (NLT)

levels of high school and the only time I entered a university was to pick up my very brainy sister from her lectures.

I intentionally had to turn my focus to what the word of God said about me and to re-read my journal notes. Both spoke loud and clear to me. Both said the same thing. "I, your God have made you, I believe in you, I chose you. I have appointed you. You are my child, you have all you need in Me."

Be intentional and fully aware when you find yourself listening to the wrong voice. That voice may be the dominant one in your head but if you tune in, you will hear the sweet soft voice of the Holy Spirit saying, "I am the truth, I am the way, listen to what I have to say about you."

His truth must be our declaration.

MY GOD IS A GOD WHO SETS THE RECORD STRAIGHT

Day 128
ARE YOU WILLING TO SWALLOW YOUR PRIDE?

It's Monday and the rent is due on Thursday! OK God, how are you going to handle this one? This was my conversation to God during the start of the first lecture for the day. As quick as a flash God said, "Sell that linen you have from Vietnam." "What God, are you kidding? These people don't have extra money to be buying linen, and why would they even want to?" I put that conversation at the back of my mind, but God kept at me and I kept arguing with Him. "Just do it," He'd keep saying. I knew it was God, without a doubt, but it seemed so ridiculous and I would be risking embarrassment in the process. Sell Vietnamese linen to Bible College students, yeah right! By the time the lecture had come to an end, I was bursting from the inside out with the compulsion that I had to do this. I turned to Paul and told him about the intense conversation I had been having with God during the morning's lecture time and in his 'whatever God says, simple faith, don't care what people think' response, answered, "Sure, if that's what God said to do." (Don't you just love Paul's attitude?)

The bell rang and Paul and I were first out of class and straight to the car to get the boxes of linen. The whole time while doing this, I was squirming and feeling totally uncomfortable about the whole process. It was only because I knew God was somehow in this that I obeyed.

We walked into the meals room (the big, wide open meals room that echoed when you spoke), with boxes in hand and began to set up our linen. While still feeling completely awkward about this whole idea, God said, "Chill Deb, don't worry, you just let the students know about the linen and I will do the rest."

By the time we had finished setting up, all the students had arrived and were getting their morning tea and chatting away to each other about their weekend's adventures.

> He said, "Throw the net off the right side of the boat and see what happens." They did what he said. All of a sudden there were so many fish in it, they weren't strong enough to pull it in.
> John 21:6 (MSG)

I took a deep breath and then in my 'not so confident' voice, said, "Excuse me everyone, if anyone is interested, we have some linen from Vietnam for sale." I smiled and quickly moved away from the table to go get my own morning tea. As Paul and I sat down to eat, I glanced through the corner of my eye to see if even just one person would find this linen remotely interesting to look at, let alone buy. I couldn't believe what I saw, not just one, but many, were gathered around the table checking out our products. One by one they started coming up to us saying, love the linen, I want to buy this one, I want to buy that one. Some said, "I want to buy but won't have money until Thursday. Will Thursday be OK to pay?" We needed fifty dollars for our rent on Thursday. That morning we sold $133 worth.

OK God, You got me!

MY GOD IS A GOD WHO WANTS US TO JUST DO WHAT HE SAYS, NO QUESTIONS ASKED

Day 129 – 132 FLOODGATES

God turned on a tap after our announcement about that linen on the Monday. From that day on until we finished college, more and more linen was sold to these precious students. Some even gave us more than the asking price. By the time we left college, we had sold almost every piece. But much more than this, that simple act of obedience opened a floodgate. Just like when those disciples let their nets down on the other side of the boat to get more fish than they could have possibly imagined, finance began to flow into our hands from all directions in many different ways.

> Jesus looked at them and said, "With man it is impossible, but not with God. For all things are possible with God."
> Mark 10:27 (ESV)

During this week alone, cheques arrived in the mail. Yes cheques! I am sure some of you will be thinking, "What are they?" Ah, the days of slow mail, and ten-day clearance of cheques! More support letters arrived from churches, money appeared in our bank and the most amazing of all, the petrol we put in our tank never ran dry.

After rent and food, we had just fifteen dollars left from the week's tablecloth enterprise so we put that in the car ready to travel up to Newcastle for the weekend. In the natural, fifteen dollars in those days would get you a quarter of a tank of petrol. The car was on empty when we arrived at the petrol station, but we put just fifteen dollars worth of petrol in believing it would get us to Newcastle. We watched the gauge go up to its usual quarter of a tank, but the further down the road we got, the higher the needle went until it reached the almost full level. We couldn't believe what we were seeing. It was simply not possible in the natural, but again, God was proving Himself to be the God of the impossible.

You have to know God is able to do abundantly more than we can ask or imagine. Trust in the Lord, not in your own understanding of how, or what, provision looks like.

**MY GOD IS THE GOD WHO SPEAKS.
EVEN THE FISH OF THE SEA OBEY HIM**

Day 133 -134 GOD WORKS WITH RUBBLE

When we see rubble, we may think, can anything come from it? But God is in the business of restoring rubble, He loves rubble, God can even build His church from rubble. Giving God our rubble changes it from a pile of rocks to an amazing masterpiece that He can use as a testament to His power and grace. That is what He does in us when we allow Him to mold us through our journey of life.

God was in the process of taking our rubble and building us with stones of resilience and strength like never before. Where there was weakness, His strength was rising in us. Where there was doubt, there was growing trust in His able-ness. Where there was a 'can we?' mindset, a 'we can' do all things through Christ who strengthens us for this journey, was forming.

> I will answer them before they even call to me. While they are still talking about their needs, I will go ahead and answer their prayers!
> Isaiah 65:24 (NLT).

This weekend saw our (well, actually my) rubble of doubt change to a cornerstone of God's able-ness once more as we waited on God to provide housing for us from the time we were to finish college until the day we would fly out. So far nothing suitable had come up to house the four of us that was rent friendly (aka free) and time was ticking by quickly!

We were visiting pastors from a supporting church over this particular weekend and Paul mentioned that we needed a place to stay. Their response was quite surprising. "Really? When do you need a house?" Paul gave them the dates and again the pastor looked stunned. "Really, we have been looking for someone to take care of our house for ages. In fact, every time we asked and set up someone to look after our home, it fell through. It was strange! Obviously God was keeping our house for you."

Able-ness. God again was proving His able-ness to us. I just love that scripture in Isaiah 65:24 (NLT) says, "I will answer them before they even call to me. While they are still talking about their needs, I will go ahead and answer their prayers!"

God help us to continue to grow in trust of Your great able-ness.

MY GOD IS A GOD WHO IS ALWAYS ONE, TWO, THREE STEPS AHEAD OF US!

Day 135 - 139 LAST WEEK OF COLLEGE

The last week of college came with feelings of both excitement and nervousness because this last week also meant we were about to jump into the first week of all things needing to come together before D Day (Departure Day).

We did however, still have this final week to conquer. In some ways, the most important of all the weeks at college. The grand finale week. The 'therefore go into all the world' week. Everyone was excited to be finally finishing the course, but sad to be saying goodbye to each other. We had journeyed together through so many good and hard times. Times of feeling overwhelmed, tired, homesick, believing God for provisions, but also great times of sharing vision, heart and love for the nations that God had planted in each of us.

> I, the Lord, have called you and given you power to see that justice is done on earth. Through you I will make a covenant with all peoples; through you I will bring light to the nations.
> Isaiah 42:6 (GNT)

Paul and I were in awe at the many nations represented in that classroom. People who had come from different nations, backgrounds, ages and circumstances, willing to let go of what was behind them to plunge into a diverse and challenging nation that lay before them. Why? Because they chose to get out of their comfort zone, out of their everyday life and say YES to God and to do whatever it took to follow His calling. We loved that! We were equally proud of each other and to this day, still have connections with some of those wonderful people who are continuing to do amazing things.

I must not forget to mention also that God continued to show up with His miraculous signs and provision each and every day this week and would you believe, even during this last week, these last days, people, including our hosts, were still buying our linen. These beautiful people we were living with during our college days, these amazing hosts who fed us and our kids, when they were with us, for free, took Belinda and Josh out, just to bless them, and were now asking could they buy our wares. And did they buy, they bought up big! I think they were buying just to help us, but hey, that's how God works. We went from several boxes of linen to almost no linen at all during our college days.

It just goes to show you God will use anything to get a job done!

MY GOD IS EVEN IN THE LINEN BUSINESS

Day 140 STEP TWO

> Keep your eyes open for God, watch for his works; be alert for signs of his presence.
> Psalm 105: 4 (MSG)

Today, we drove out of the driveway of our hosts' home for the last time and took the final trip from Sydney to Newcastle as college graduates.

We now had two places secured for us to live from today until we boarded our plane. On opening the door to our first home we were welcomed with a house full of groceries and supplies. Miracle provision never stopped flowing. We had put twenty dollars worth of petrol in our car to get from point A to B and were handed twenty dollars in cash on arrival.

We could have been handed a hundred dollars on that day, but I am glad it was twenty dollars. The significance of it being the exact amount we put into our car spoke louder because again, God was saying, I see absolutely everything. I am in your every little detail, every minute need with one hundred percent precision. Stay watchful for the little but very significant interventions from God.

MY GOD IS PLEASED WHEN WE NOTICE HIS WORKS

Day 141 GOING BEFORE DECISION MAKERS

Today the fearless field leader at the time, Tom Rawls was meeting with the authorities of Vietnam to gain visas for us.

Before we had officially applied to become missionaries with our mission arm of our church movement, Australia Christian Churches, they had requested visas for another couple to go into Vietnam, but it was flatly denied. However, this didn't phase us as we knew in our hearts, God was with us and His favour was on us. Without a doubt, we knew God was leading us and the visas were already approved in the heavenlies. Just like in Isaiah 65:24, God had already done what needed to be done in the hearts of the decision makers, the rest would be a formality. Our job was to pray and trust Him.

So what did that say for the couple who were denied visas? That they were not good enough, spiritual enough, equipped enough? No, not at all! In fact, this couple, were a role model couple of godliness and much more experienced than we were at this moment in time, but God had other plans for them. They had already been working in another country, but that season had come to an end for them, which meant they were available to go wherever they were needed. They saw Vietnam as an opportunity, a possible open door, but God was saying, "No" because He wanted them elsewhere. Jeremiah 29:11 (NIV) says, "For I know the plans that I have for you." Keep your heart open and your ear attuned to My whisper and you will see the plans I have for you are tailor made for you." God directed this beautiful couple to Mozambique and they began a very fruitful ministry there that continues to this day.

> I see what you've done. Now see what I've done. I've opened a door before you that no one can slam shut. You don't have much strength, I know that; you used what you had to keep My Word. You didn't deny me when times were rough.
> Revelation 3:8 (MSG)

MY GOD HAS THE LAST WORD. HE IS THE DECISION MAKER

Day 142 – 147 PULLING OUT ALL STOPS

We had been working on raising support during our college days, but as you can imagine, it was not easy juggling study, visits to see our children and working on building our partnership base from campus. Now we had a clear run, we had to pull out all stops. With just over seven weeks before departing our familiar shores to the relatively unknown, we were racing to the finish line. Despite the sense of urgency we had, there was still the need to approach this last lap of this particular circuit with the James 2:22 principle. Doing everything in our power we could do and leaning on God to do what only He could do.

Much of what was to be done was very administrative. Phone calls, writing newsletters, sending further support letters out and ticking off our to do list, making sure we hadn't missed anything.

No matter what our occupation, abilities or calling is in life, we cannot get away from the tyranny of administration. Those of you who have the luxury of a personal assistant know there is still no escape from some administrative duties. I am sure doctors didn't sign up for administration when they were studying medicine at university. Their desire was to give practical assistance for the wellbeing of the sick, yet even they cannot avoid the patient's diagnosis write ups, referrals and prescriptions that they must do daily.

Why am I going on about administration? Well frankly, it's because to do anything well, and have long term partnerships and connections, it's going to take effort on our part, even in the things we don't naturally lean towards. Whether we like it or not, administrating our call, ministry, work or life in general, is a God requirement so that we stay in touch and accountable for all that we do.

> For the administration of this service not only supplies the needs of the saints, but also is abounding through many thanksgivings to God
> 2Cor 9:12 (NKJV)

Sometimes we didn't feel like making that call or writing one more letter, but we did it and it paid off. Our support came in very quickly compared to most who were raising funds for the field and it was because we were diligent in administrating our call.

MY GOD HONOURS THOSE WHO ARE HONOURABLE

Day 148   I SAID EVERYDAY

"We made a pact God, you and I, remember? I said every day, Lord."

Today was Sunday and we were given a great opportunity to share our vision at our home church in Newcastle. The service was great, lunch and the company afterwards was fabulous and the evening service was equally wonderful, but there was nothing on this day that I could point to and say, "There it is, our today's God moment." Nothing. Because we'd been out all day, we were glad to get home and unwind before bed. However, we had determined in our hearts, we would not lay down until God turned up, but already, it was very late.

> Let us hold fast the confession of our hope without wavering, for he who promised is faithful.
> Hebrews 10:23 (NKJV)
> In other words, Daddy promised,
> Daddy will deliver!

I remember this night so clearly. As a family, we prayed a very spiritual prayer, "God You said, You promised, thank you, amen." We believed He could, and would do something, but didn't know what or how at this late hour. So we sat and we waited. Every minute seemed more like ten, but at 10:40pm the phone rang and before we even answered the call, we knew, God was about to show up.

I picked up the phone and it was a family we knew from church. "Hi Deb, sorry to ring so late, we weren't sure if you would be still up, in fact we were going to leave it until tomorrow to ring you, but we felt we needed to ring you tonight, hope you don't mind. We wanted to let you know, that as a family, we are going to support you in your ministry every month." And there it was! Thank you, Jesus!

> "Know therefore that the LORD your God is God, the faithful God who keeps covenant and steadfast love with those who love him and keep his commandments, to a thousand generations." Deuteronomy 7:9 (ESV)

Even though we had prayed that prayer of reminder to God, we knew in our spirit, before midnight struck, God would fulfill His promise. You may ask, how could you have that kind of assurance? This kind of assurance comes by daily putting off the adult rationale and putting on the child-like faith. The type of faith that says; "Daddy promised, so Daddy will deliver."

We love to adult-ise how things will happen, but God expects us to grow up and become child-like in our faith, which is the only way to please Him.

The other reason I had assurance was because, the more I travelled along this journey, the deeper my sense of His awareness became. It was like I was swimming in a deep vast ocean and whatever direction I swam, I would still be surrounded by water. God was all around me and I knew it. He was around our family. He'd never left us.

I have often said throughout this book, trust God in your journey, but the only way you can truly understand that trust, is by learning from a child-like perspective. A child believes without question their parent is going to deliver on what they promise. Even though at times a parent may disappoint, (and we have all done that), the child continues to believe in the parent's promises. How much more can we trust in a Holy God who says, "If you then, though you are evil, know how to give good gifts to your children, how much more will I, your Heavenly Father give the Holy Spirit to those who ask him!" Luke 11:13 (NIV)

He doesn't say, check your circumstances first, or pray for several hours to get my attention, He says know! Know who I am and who I am to you, your Daddy. And a child doesn't try to be the son and daughter of his or her parent, they just are! You don't have to try to be a child of God, you walk in that and then He will deliver the best for you.

BE ASSURED AS I AM, MY GOD, IS A GOD OF PROMISE

Day 149   CERTIFICATE IN HAND

Today our second 'passport' arrived which would allow us entrance into Vietnam. That all important TESOL certificate. The piece of paper that the Government of Vietnam had agreed would allow us into the country.

To hold this physical qualification in my hand reminded me of all the hard work I had put in to gain this baby. It also reminded me of where I had come from. As I have previously mentioned, the last day of school, was my best day of school, just scraping through to gain my high school certificate. So today was a proud moment for me. It smashed any self-talk or enemy whisper of, "You are not smart enough." I can now hold this piece of paper up high and say to the world, "Just take a look at this!"

> Not that we are competent in ourselves to claim anything for ourselves, but our competence comes from God.
> 2 Corinthians 3:5 (NIV)

MY GOD IS A GOD WHO HAS ALWAYS QUALIFIED ME

Day 150 – 155   DANCING SHOES

I never used to like shoes. I used to say, it would be great if shoes were never invented. For years in fact, I only ever owned one pair of shoes because I thought, that is all you need to get around. You may be thinking (if you are a guy), right on Deb, that is all you need! Yes, boys, but we are girls. However, in the past I would have agreed with you wholeheartedly. In fact, I cared so little about shoes that I hadn't even noticed that my one and only pair, which I wore for every occasion, were totally worn out, and really quite unacceptable to be wearing when standing on the platform speaking in front of people. I am not saying you have to be showy or anything, but these shoes screamed, "Send me to the bin!"

It only came to my attention when the pastor's wife at the church I was speaking at, came up to me after the service and said she would love to take me shoe shopping as she could see I desperately needed a new pair of shoes.

> And to her it was granted to be arrayed in fine linen, clean and bright, for the fine linen is the righteous acts of the saints.
> Rev 19:8 (NKJV)

As she was telling me this, I found myself looking down at my old faithfuls and for the first time, I noticed the true state of what resembled dog's tongues flapping around my feet. OK, maybe not that bad, but yeek, they were not a pretty sight. To me they were still working and that's all that mattered. It took someone else to help me see the need I had. That I indeed needed a new pair of shoes and I needed them now!

You know God not only answers prayers we are aware of, but He also answers ones we are not aware of and He does it all the time. Just think of the many times you just missed that car, or almost dropped that precious ring down the sink or you felt to turn around and found you were just in time to catch your child as they were falling. They are all God answered prayers before we realised we needed them answered.
As Isaiah 65:24 (NIV) says, "Before they call I will answer; while they are still speaking I will hear." This scripture is kind of funny in my situation, because it was while I was literally still speaking, that God spoke to the pastor's wife and told her, "Go get that poor girl some new shoes and fast!"

New shoes were just one of the many incredible blessings God gave me that week and gave us as a family. Every day, finance flowed in from all over the place like never before. God was moving things along faster now and the urgency of being fully prepared was tangibly upon us. It was both exciting and scary at the same time. This is what saying YES to God will do. You will be exhilarated and nervous, but know God's got you!

MY GOD IS EVEN IN THE SHOE BUSINESS

Day 156 BE STRONG AND COURAGEOUS

> Yes, be bold and strong! Banish fear and doubt! For remember, the Lord your God is with you wherever you go."
> Joshua 1:9 (TLB)

These were the first words God spoke to Joshua as he took the reins from Moses. When Joshua got this word from God, to be strong and courageous in Joshua 1:6-7, God told Joshua not once but three times. And each time, He was telling Joshua, something specific. Be strong and courageous, because you will lead My people into the land of their inheritance. Be strong and very courageous, make sure you don't veer from the mandate I am giving you. Be strong and courageous, there will be times you may feel afraid or discouraged, but I am telling you, don't be afraid or get discouraged because I am walking this journey with you. When God says something more than once, we need to take very careful note of what He is saying and understanding there will be a place and time when we will need to refer back to that word.

This morning as I woke, those very words were on my heart and as I opened the Bible to read the verses they came from, I was drawn to the fact that God had said to Joshua on the second time to "Be strong and very courageous." We had no idea what the 'very' would mean to us in the future, but didn't feel overly concerned because we thought our mandate was to serve another couple.

When God said to Joshua, be strong and courageous the first time, He was wanting Joshua to be confident in taking these reins of leadership. Joshua had been made ready to lead God's people into their promised land.

Lead God's people. A big ask! We had no idea at this time that our mandate of serving another couple was going to change completely as soon as we got to our field. We had no clue that God was actually setting us up to take the reins of leadership from the couple we expected to serve. No wonder He woke me with those words.

My point here is that we need to pay close attention to God when He speaks so directly to us in this manner. We need to scribe those words deep in our heart for three reasons:

1. For you to be at peace with it, knowing God has gone ahead of you.
2. It is for a purpose. He is preparing you in His plan for your life.
3. He chose you because He knows what you are made of and that you are up for the task. Be strong and courageous.

MY GOD IS OUR STRENGTH AND COURAGE

Day 157 – 163 DAYS OF GRACE

Through these several days, God was graciously giving us a rest from the effort of our running around support raising. It was nice to stop for a brief time to catch our breath and rest. Yet, during these days of us putting our feet up, God continued to show up, on our behalf. The right amount of money came into our hands on the right day, to pay the bill that was due that day. We just happened to meet a Vietnamese girl on the streets of Newcastle and connected instantly. This was unusual because Newcastle had very few Vietnamese at that time. We received phone call after phone call from churches confirming support, and our hosts called us in to let us know that we could be assured of a place to stay until we got on that plane.

Sometimes, actually most times, God is expecting us to apply James 2:22, but there are times He says, sit for a while, rest, leave it all to me because I never sleep or slumber.

> He will never let me stumble, slip, or fall. For he is always watching, never sleeping. Psalm 121:3-4 (TLB)

God is telling us, "While you rest, I will keep the wheels rolling, just watch me."

MY GOD IS A GOD OF THE RHYTHM OF GRACE

Day 164 IT'S A YES!

That long awaited confirmation we had been waiting for came today! Yes, send them in. You are invited. Please be informed. I'd like to welcome you. Our country of destiny had finally given us the green light to come in. Now all that was left to do were a few minor details such as raising money for airfares, visas, vaccinations and the rest of our support. Easy!

While we were experiencing the rhythms of grace, and resting; God was of course, going about the business of working with the authorities of our new adopted country, whispering in their ears, "Pick up that red stamp, put it on the Hilton's paperwork and be ready to say yes when ACCI Australia calls one more time to again ask if we are done yet."

**MY GOD WHO DIRECTS THE WIND AND THE SEA,
CAN DIRECT LEADERS OF A NATION**

Day 165   GET IT OUT OF THE BIN

> In view of all this, what can we say? If God is for us, who can be against us?
> Romans 8:31 (GNT)

All our requests for support were sent out, we had followed up everyone as much as we could and now it was time to wait.

One church we had written to had an 'only project support' policy. This church was, and is, a very passionate mission church and they always gave very sacrificially in many areas, but did not support individual missionaries. We knew that, but God spoke clearly to Paul, and said, "Write to them anyway."

When their email popped up on our screen today we weren't sure what it would say. However, we had a quiet confidence that it would have a yes attached to it because God had already told us to act. We again had said YES to God in a situation where facts said otherwise.

Dear Paul and Deb,

Well today, as a board, we have decided to support you personally.

We want to let you know that this is not something we usually do as a church. In fact, whenever I, as the Missions Pastor, receive requests for personal missionary support (and we get many), I discard them. It was no different when I received your letter of request. As soon as I recognised yours as yet another request for support, I did what I always did and threw it in the bin!

Your letter had no sooner touched the sides of the can when God spoke to me very clearly and said, 'Get that letter out of the bin and support these people.' I then had to take your letter to our senior pastor to present your case. I told him that I felt we should support you and his response was, "You know we don't support missionaries personally." But after I explained what had happened, he replied, "God is in this, we must support them."

We look forward to our partnership.

Signed the Mission Pastor.

Amazing ay!

MY GOD IS A GOD WHO WORKS OUTSIDE THE BOX

Day 166 – 168
BEING WILLING TO DO WHATEVER IT TAKES

Sometimes you have to be willing to pull up your sleeves and do whatever it takes to get to where you are going. An opportunity came up for Paul to clean up someone's yard for cash in hand. Of course Paul said yes straight away but when we visited the place to assess the work, we found the yard was slightly bigger than your average garden and it looked like it hadn't been touched in years. I would say it resembled more of a jungle than a backyard. This was not going to be a one man job, so our kids and I agreed that we needed to get in and help Paul do this not so-little clean up job. It was hard work, the day was long and the heat was unrelenting. We got tired,

> God blesses those who are humble, for they will inherit the whole earth
> Matthew 5:5 (NLT)

scratched with thorns and bitten by ants, but we persevered because this job gave us another stone in our sling to catapult us into our new season, which was virtually upon us.

Paul was also asked to help with other labouring jobs during this season and of course his answer was always YES. Our YES to God needs to be a YES no matter what that looks like. Sometimes it will appear in pretty packages, like when unexpected money turns up in your bank account. Other times it will look like dirty paper bags, as in this difficult backyard clean up. But we have learnt from walking this journey of trust that if God is in it, no matter how it is presented, inside will always be gold, gold that will benefit and grow us. We must be willing to unwrap the opportunity, engage with it and let God take care of the outcome.

We can never be too proud to say YES to things that seem below us or become big-headed when things are just handed to us. Either end of the spectrum, God wants us to stay humble, and right hearted, with an attitude of gratitude.

MY GOD IS A GOD WHO HUMBLED HIMSELF FOR US

Day 169 THE EXACT MOMENT

Have you ever walked into a situation and known that if you hadn't turned up at that exact moment, you would have missed an incredible opportunity?

Well, that is exactly what happened to us when we walked into the home of the hosts who took care of us during our World Harvest Institute college days. We had wanted to visit this lovely family one more time before leaving our Australian shores so we chose this day to visit. We pulled up into their driveway,

> There is a season (a time appointed) for everything and a time for every delight and event or purpose under heaven
> Ecclesiastes 3:1 (AMP)

knocked on their door, and as they opened it to us, their phone rang. Our host ran to answer it, quickly returning to us to say, "How strange, this phone call is for you." We had not been living here, or even been in contact, for over two months, yet literally the moment we walk back into these people's lives, the phone rings in their house and it is for us. Coincidence? I don't think so!

The conversation with the person on the other end of the phone began, "Hi this is Pastor Russell, I thought I would ring you today to chat to you about our church supporting your family. This was the only contact phone number I had for you so I thought I would give it a shot." I would call that a bulls-eye shot!

This particular church turned out to be one of our very significant partners as it is one of the very few who have been supporting us continually since the beginning and still today, are highly engaged in all that we do. That is called partnership.

MY GOD IS A GOD WHO CAUSES WORLDS TO COLLIDE

Day 170 – 180
MOMENTUM

When I think of momentum, I think of traction and I liken traction to those little cars kids play with. You know, those little cars you have to pull back several times in order for them to go forward. Children just love them and will do this over and over again, pulling back, letting go and then watching how far they travel each time. They don't think about the work they have to do to see the results because the outcome far out weighs the effort put in.

Sometimes while on our journey to get where we are going, all we can feel is the traction, the tension, the pullback, but God keeps whispering in our ear, keep going, keep going, keep going and then one day, He says ok, let go, and whoa! You are catapulted down the track with great speed. Things start to gain momentum and you will watch it with great excitement, just like those children who jump for joy when they see the

> And let us not get tired of doing what is right, (the traction) for after a while we will reap a harvest of blessing if we don't get discouraged and give up (the momentum).
> Galatians 6:9 (TLB)

car go all the way to the end of their hallway.

We had been doing a lot of pulling and waiting, and being satisfied with seeing a grain of promise, but then God spoke with action as if to say, "OK, let go of the car now. I want to show you how far you have actually come on this journey."

During these weeks, so many things came together and we saw tangibly the workings of God behind the scenes. Finance had been sent to our missions agency for airfares which meant we could now book our tickets, as well as further monthly support, but the best news of all, those all important visas came through.

I have to say, these days getting a visa to travel into Vietnam is quite easy, but this was not the case in 1998. They did not just hand them out to 'whosoever will' back then, and when they did choose to give someone that golden ticket, it came with a lot of red tape. Even for tourists, it was not a quick turn around, so for us, having to wait and go through the process of being checked out thoroughly several times, visa approval was definitely a significant achievement.

Over these ten days, God also gave us an incredible promise from Haggai 2:19 (NIV) "From this day on, I will bless you." You maybe saying, "What do you mean, from this day on? Hasn't God been blessing you all along?" Yes, God was definitely blessing us throughout this journey of faith as you have read, but what He was telling us at this point in time was, "This car your are in, is now running at full speed and your traction time is over. Your car is going all the way to the end of your hallway and beyond."

MY GOD GIVES MOMENTUM TO THOSE WHO SUCCESSFULLY WORK THROUGH THE TRACTION

Day 181
REMEMBER WHAT I ASKED GOD FOR?

"God will you do this for me? Will you, from this day, today, until we board that plane for Vietnam show me something, anything, every day, a miracle, from you, that says, 'Deb, you and your family are on the right track in this new venture. This is your destiny and you can trust me.'"

And so here we are, with just two weeks to go until we board the plane. Did we ever think we would get this far? In the natural, maybe not, but having God show up in my life every day, made it possible. Today being significant in the fact that on this day six months ago I prayed this prayer to God, I wanted to remind you that God hears your prayers. I feel I need to say that again. God really does hear your prayers. Take it from me, or better still, take it from the Word of God, God listens and He responds.

Here is proof, He really is listening to you.

> Psalm 65:2 (TLB) And because you answer prayer, all mankind will come to you with their requests.
> Psalm 34:15 (NSAB) The eyes of the Lord are toward the righteous and His ears are open to their cry.
> Proverbs 15:29 (MSG) God keeps his distance from the wicked but He closely attends to the prayers of God-loyal people.
>
> Psalm 66:19-20 (NASB) But certainly God has heard; He has given heed to the voice of my prayer. Blessed be God, Who has not turned away my prayer nor His loving kindness from me.

See... I told you...

MY GOD IS FAITHFULLY LISTENING AND ATTENDING TO OUR PRAYERS

Day 182 LOCK IN THE DATE

Trusting God in your journey, saying YES to each step is key to arriving at the destined place God is calling you to, but one major step in turning that key is definitely setting a date. You can be sharing your call, your vision, your purpose and preparing all you need to, but still be sitting in a comfortable position because you haven't nailed your colours to the mast when it comes to defining your D Day, the date you will step into what you have been preparing for all this time. There is absolutely no risk or faith in that. At some point, you are going to have to put a stamp on a day and let the world know, this is it. In some ways it is easier doing all the things you need to do in preparation, than actually declaring to one and all you will be leaving, moving, changing or stepping into what

God has purposed you to do on such and such date, because once you do that, you are saying I am fully engaged to the point of jumping in, trusting God that what He spoke to me about will now come to pass.

As a family we made a decision to mark a day and share our news even though, at this point we still needed half an airfare and a further $200 monthly support. We were fully leaning in to Him now to finish what He started.

When you set your date, you can be sure, not all your ducks will be lined up in a row, but you should be well and truly certain this is a God thing by now so go ahead and mark your day. Don't worry about those ducks because the Holy Spirit is the duck whisperer and He will get them lined up at the right time.

MY GOD LOVES SPEAKING TO DUCKS

Day 183 FAMILY

I have said it before, but I will say it again because I believe it is important for you to hear. If you are called as a family, God considers the whole family. He is not one to call just you and hope your kids fit in. Surprise, surprise, He is calling your kids too. He has a purpose for them also in the measure He has given. Don't worry about your kids.

And if you are single, going out on your own, you have to know God's watching over your loved ones that are waving you off and He will bless them for the sacrifice.

> For the promise is for you and for your children and for all who are far off, everyone whom the Lord our God calls to himself.
> Acts 2:39 (ESV)

For us as a family, we were going as a team. What God called Paul and I to, He was also calling our kids to. Today was real confirmation of this when each one of us were prophesied over. Not that we hang our hats on prophesies, but seeing our kids be acknowledged by God as individuals, not just as family members, was thrilling for us as parents.

The word for our daughter, Belinda was that she would make significant friendships and that is what she did. Belinda began a street children's ministry that went on to see her train and teach these youth in skills to gain employment.

The word to Josh, our son, was that he would also play a significant role. By just being himself, he would make an impact, pray for people and they would be healed. Josh is a magnet. People are always drawn to him.

Whether your children are teenagers or just toddlers, be assured God's got them in mind and they will play a role in whatever you do.

And today, we received a further fifty dollars monthly support. Yay, only $150 to go!

BE ASSURED! GOD'S PROMISES ARE FOR YOU AND YOUR FAMILY

Day 184 -187
MORE PEOPLE ARE ON BOARD THAN YOU THINK!

You will find there are times when sharing your vision with people that some seem completely disinterested in what you have to say, even to the point of interrupting you to tell you about the latest new thing they have just bought. It can make you mad sometimes, and you find yourself wanting to give them a big lecture about focusing on God things rather than their latest car, but we cannot do that. Their journey is not our journey, we must not judge, because that is not our job. Leave their journey to God and just love on them anyway.

Then we find people who have not only been interested in what we are about to embark on, but have actually been thinking of how they can help. During these past few days, we were caught by surprise with just how many people had been doing just that. We had offers from people wanting to drive us to the airport. Others came up with contacts for when we arrived in Vietnam so we wouldn't feel alone or disconnected. People rang us to say God had had them raising money for us over a period of time and they were now sending it to us so we were not going into Vietnam empty handed. One friend even rang us to say he had been working on selling Paul's wetsuit and had finally got us a sale. And the list went on. Some people did little things for us while others sacrificed big by being willing to get up at an unearthly hour to drive in the busy Sydney traffic from Newcastle at 4:30am, 160 kilometres each way. All these things fed our spirit and filled our love tank. We weren't going to Vietnam alone, but with arms held high by many people.

The strength of friendship is invaluable, especially when you are doing something out of the norm! Many of these beautiful people are still in the trenches with us today. Love people and you will find people loving you back.

> So Joshua fought the Amalekites as Moses had ordered, and Moses, Aaron and Hur went to the top of the hill. As long as Moses held up his hands, the Israelites were winning, but whenever he lowered his hands, the Amalekites were winning. When Moses' hands grew tired, they took a stone and put it under him and he sat on it. Aaron and Hur held his hands up one on one side, one on the other so that his hands remained steady till sunset. So Joshua overcame the Amalekite army with the sword.
> Exodus 17:10-13 (NIV)

We cannot concern ourselves with those who do not understand or think we are crazy, but keep our eyes on the One who is always championing us on, Jesus Christ, and thank Him for all those wonderful friends He puts in our path. Jesus knows the struggles we go through on the journey, so He gathers an army to hold our hands up high when we get tired to win every battle to get to the finish line.

MY GOD IS A GOD WHO GATHERS OUR ARMY

Day 188   YOU'VE GOT TO READ THIS!

We had just checked our bank account to see if funds had come through for our airfares before heading off to the travel agency to pay for our tickets. Disappointingly, the cupboard was bare. The travel agency had informed us the last time we met that we needed to pay for our airfares by the following week. That was this week, today in fact. The money had been promised to us by our supporters, yet none had appeared in our bank thus far. We needed to talk to our travel agent to see if we could pay just before leaving rather than this week, but when we suggested this to her, she told us, "If you don't pay today, you could lose your tickets."

We came out of the travel agency and sat on a bench seat situated just in front, feeling very despondent. Right there, amongst the crowds of shoppers, we cried out to God, "Lord what should we do?" As soon as we finished praying that prayer, Paul said, "I am going to go back to the bank and check the account." I said, "You're crazy, we've just been to the bank." He said "Deb, I know, but I am going." He was gone for ten whole minutes, which seemed like forever as

> Everyone was amazed and gave praise to God. They were filled with awe and said, "We have seen remarkable things today."
> Luke 5:26 (NIV)

Belinda, Josh and I waited on that seat. On his return, his face said it all. No money right! I thought to myself, "ok God, now what?" Then he pulled from his back pocket a white slip of paper. On the top of that paper was the name of our bank and printed under that were our names and below that, a figure I couldn't believe! Clear as day, in black and white on that beautiful piece of paper, was more than enough to pay our airfares! Right there and then we jumped up and down and raced straight back into the agency where we presented our cheque for the full amount to a stunned travel agent.

Do you want to praise Him with me right now? That's our God!

MY GOD IS A GOD WHO NEVER DISAPPOINTS

DAY 189-190
FINAL WEEKEND LIVING IN AUSSIE LAND

It's hard to believe that this time next week, we will be putting on a new coat. The coat of a foreigner. Living in a land not our own, but a land that would soon become our heartland, Vietnam.

> Hear, O Israel! The Lord is our God, the Lord is one [the only God]! You shall love the Lord your God with all your heart and mind and with all your soul and with all your strength [your entire being]. These words, which I am commanding you today, shall be [written] on your heart and mind.
> Deut 6:4-6 (AMP)

We wanted to savour this weekend, enjoy everything it had to offer. Spend time with our family and friends who we were about to leave, take one more stroll around the shopping centres that were non-existent in Vietnam and eat more lamb. But the most important thing we wanted to do above all else, was to suck everything out of the final body of Christ gathering on our last Sunday in Australia, where we could freely meet together to pray and worship God, something that was not so easily attainable in the land we were entering. Understanding this reality, we realised how much we all take for granted in our homeland, privileged to experience such freedom without restraints.

We were blessed beyond measure this weekend from so many and further words of prophesy flowed into our hearts that filled us for the journey ahead. Unspeakable joy came down from heaven over us, touching our spirits, causing us to soar. God was readying us!

Never take for granted the liberties we have. Although times are changing in Australia now, we continue to have many freedoms available to us that still, so many do not. Freedom to worship God in our homes and our churches.

MY GOD IS A GOD WHO REMINDS US TO BE GRATEFUL AND NOT TO TAKE HIM FOR GRANTED

Day 191 – 194 ALL SYSTEMS GO

It was our final few days before leaving, but there was still much to do including a few last minute jobs for people to earn some much needed money.

Saying YES to God came with lots of opportunities. During this last week, we were given some night work at a local supermarket to pack shelves. This was a job neither of us had ever done before, but we were willing to do it. It was actually lots of fun and it didn't feel like work at all. Stacking shelves and making sure everything lined up in perfect order also fed my tendency for wanting to have everything in its place. During these last few days the rest of the money came in for our support, just in time! Would you believe it? Of course you would. You must know by now it's all about these two ingredients I have been trying to get you to hear throughout this book. Live by the promise we have in James 2:22, works and faith mixed together will bring results, and let your default answer to God always be YES.

Just see what God will do in your life with these two ingredients. You can't lose!

MY GOD IS A GOD WHO WILL PROVIDE AND GUIDE IF WE ARE WILLING TO SAY YES

Day 195 OH MY GOODNESS, HERE WE GO!

The date is the 3rd April, 1998 and the time is 4.30am. We are dressed, packed and ready to go. Our faithful, get up at the crack of dawn to drive 160 kilometres and home again friend Gary, had arrived and was ready to take us to the airport. Everything was now go!

The excitement in the air was tangible. Our time had finally come. All the preparation, all the fundraising, all the running around the country, all the manual labour we did as a family to raise money, all the stretching of believing for another day to get us to this point was now behind us. We had said our goodbyes, leaving the all familiar and family behind as we drove away, with the future before us.

At around 7am we arrived at the airport, checked our bags in and before we knew it we were sitting on the plane, the plane that would take us to our God orchestrated, long planned, life changing, destined purpose. The aircraft raced down the runway and thrust into the air, kissing the ground goodbye with its back wheels and as we watched the landscape of Sydney fade into the distance, before turning back in our seats, we bade farewell to this, our great southland.

A couple of hours had passed when we heard the voice of the pilot introducing himself and giving us an update of where we were, "Good morning everyone, this is the captain speaking. We are crossing Central Australia right now and if you look to your left, you will see our famous Uluru also known as Ayers Rock."

Uluru, one of Australia's well known landmarks. A large red sandstone rock formation that stands at 318 metres high and 8 kilometres around. In all our life, living in Australia, we had never seen this place. A rock that drew a multitude of tourists from all around the world every year, and now, as we leave this country we've called home, we get a glimpse of this amazing natural wonder, just one of the many in this land down under. A surreal moment for us right then.

A few more hours passed and as I sat in our one way ticketed seats to Vietnam, I looked across at my family and a wave of satisfaction came over me. We were doing this journey together.

I then looked out the window to see the last slice of Australian soil passing under us, with nothing but ocean before us and without warning, it hit me. Fear! Here I was, just seconds ago, sitting in a moment of completeness and now I am having a mini stroke. I can't say whether this feeling came upon me because I was seeing that last morsel of known soil pass under me or simply because reality had started to set in. Deb, this is not some extended holiday you are going on, this is for life, as long as God asks of you. Are you ready for this? Deb, what are you doing? I was not expecting those thoughts to rise up inside of me. We were one hundred and ten percent committed, excited and expectant and yet right then, doubt came crashing in on my parade. We were no longer on the slow train that stopped at many stations, the train we wanted to go faster for so long, to get to our destiny and future. No, we were now on the fast train that was non-stop directly to our soon to be 'now' life. No

> We can be right in the middle of God's perfect will and timing and still have thoughts of, what am I doing, am I ready for this?

longer a future thing, but a living, breathing, every day life reality.

We can be right in the middle of God's perfect will and timing and still have thoughts of, what am I doing, am I ready for this? Those thoughts are OK when you know it is a God idea, not just a good idea because it is in knowing that, which will get you through those anxious times.

The panic was only for a moment because what rose up within me was all God had taught me over the past almost two hundred days and His promise in Jeremiah 29:11 (NIV) "For I know the plans I have for you," declares the Lord, "Plans to prosper you and not to harm you, plans to give you hope and a future."

Yes, His word, forever true. His word rising up within me, made everything alright again. I could nestle back down in my seat again, smile big at God and relax.

MY GOD IS A GOD WHO IS THE BRIDGE ACROSS SEASONS

Day 196-200 ARRIVED

And just like that, in just nine short (OK, it didn't feel short) hours, we arrived. It was hot, it was humid, it was crowded, noisy and chaotic, and it was wonderful. We had finally made it. The miracle journey complete! Today, we had entered our mission field. Another beginning and another miracle journey about to start.

The final five days to finish the 200-day miracle journey came with the beginnings of walking our destiny.

Every step we took over these initial five days, God was saying, "I put you here, I planted you here and it was I who made this a reality. Because you worked with me, I could get things done behind the scenes, things you don't know about. Behind the scenes I fought spiritual battles for you, whispered your name to many, as people were placed in your pathway, I guided your footsteps, I challenged your thinking, I stayed silent for you to come after Me, I fashioned you through fire, I wrapped my arms around you in the times you cried out, I caused ridiculous things to be used to provide for you (linen) and through it all, you stayed the course. What stands before Me, your God, your Father, are the results. You have been made whole, more confident, stronger, more courageous, more open and willing to do whatever it takes and now you have reached this time, your 'such a time as this' time, watch what I am going to do through you over the coming days, months and years because you said YES at every turn. Despite your doubts and fears, you continued to walk forward, believing Me above every challenge, opposition, inhibition and constraint. I, your God, am pleased with you."

Over 200 days, miracles had taken place for the glory of His Name. The Lord Jesus Christ, my God, my Saviour, my trusted friend. Loving Him and serving Him for all of my days, is a great privilege.

Now, a new season had begun, a season that has thus far lasted eighteen highly eventful years and there is so much to tell you about that!

But that, my friend, is a whole other story.

**MY GOD, MY FATHER, MY SAVIOUR,
MY COMFORTER, MY ALL**

DON'T SKIP THE EPILOGUE

To get where we want to be, to achieve what we want to achieve, we have to be willing to go through those sometimes mundane, not so fun, pushing through moments, hours, days, weeks and sometimes longer to see what is in your mind's eye become a reality. It won't happen by wishing, nor by simply praying. It takes work, hard work, trust and faith in times that are seemingly fruitless, believing that in the heavenlies, mighty things are happening on your behalf.

Each one of us has purpose. No one is exempt. We are born with purpose, with a reason to be on this earth. George Washington Carver wrote, "No individual has any right to come into the world and go out of it without leaving behind him distinct and legitimate reasons for having passed through it." I agree. This world is better off when we fulfill our God given mandate to be on this earth.

You may say, "I can't go to the mission field," but let me ask you a question. You can't go, won't go or are not called to go? There is a big difference. If you are not called to go, you are not meant to go, but you are still not meant to do nothing.

A girl came up to me one Sunday after speaking at a church in Australia. She said. "I have to tell you something. Last time you spoke at our church, you shared about your life, your journey of trust and what you are doing now, and as you were speaking I said to myself, if she can do it, I can do it." She went on to say, "Tonight you are going to see a miracle. For years, I have sat up the back of the church desperately wanting to be on stage singing, but too scared to do it. But when you shared, my fear broke and I knew that night, if God can use ordinary people like you, to do extraordinary things, He can use me to sing. That gave me the confidence to speak out about my call and I joined the church band."

YES, she got it! Exactly what I have been trying to say all along. We are all purposed. Just say YES, God's got your back and everything else. That night I watched her sing her heart out and it made me a proud mama.

Years ago, a lady from our home church was at a missions seminar. During one of the meetings, the speaker asked everyone to bow their heads and pray and ask God to speak to them right then and there about what He would want them to do in missions. As this lady began to pray, God showed her a picture of Vietnam. Her first thought was, "Vietnam? God I am only a hairdresser. How can I be used in missions as a hairdresser?" She felt both excited and puzzled.

Within weeks of that vision, Paul and I returned to Australia to visit churches and family. I desperately needed to get my hair done. Vietnamese were not used to blondes, so to say I had been living with a bad haircut was an understatement. I asked our pastor if he knew somewhere I could get my hair cut and coloured at a reasonable cost and he introduced me to none other than this lady who had received the word from God about Vietnam. The next day I was at Karin's home where she had her salon. She couldn't believe someone from Vietnam was coming and when I arrived, she launched straight into telling me what God had been speaking to her about and how baffled she was to think she could possibly be used in her profession. I also could not believe what I was hearing.

At that time, we were working with a Safe House, in Vietnam, a home for street youth. We wanted these young people to get some kind of trade so they could become self-sufficient. We did not want them living forever in an institution type environment. When asking the girls what their dream job was, some of the girls said they really wanted to set up a hairdressing salon but didn't know how they were going to do this because, for one, they had no money to train and secondly, the local hairdressers in town (at the time), had only very basic hairdressing skills themselves. When I shared this with Karin, she was floored. We both were, but again God had caused worlds to collide.

Within months of that God ordained meeting, Karin arrived with two other hairdressers and together, they trained several girls, created a space in the Street Children's Home to set up a salon, decorated it, and blessed them each with a starter kit.

Don't ever say I am just a…! God wants to use what He has put in your hands already. That gifting, passion, skill. He will take your mustard seed and create a mighty big tree for others to glean from.

So how about it? It's time to get up out of that chair, that comfortable mundane place, and start moving towards that something God has laid on your heart. It is not too late. As long as you have breath in your lungs, it is never too late.

I will stand and applaud you, but heaven will clap ever so louder when you finally rise up and say, "I am uncomfortable, I am scared, I don't know how this will work out, but I trust you God, to fulfill what you are calling me to do in my life. Let's go. I choose to say YES."

If a reoccurring passion continues to invade your mind and you're not doing it, don't waste another moment. Don't be one to look back and say I wish I had, but stand proud and say I'm glad I did.

- Deb Hilton

Now you have finished reading this book, I would love to hear your testimony of how you drew a line in the sand and said, "No more. No more wishing, hoping, dreaming, but standing up, doing, walking and living my destiny."

You can contact me on my Facebook page:
https://www.facebook.com/IsayYES/

REFERENCE NOTES

Introduction – page 7
Survey of over 90 yr olds
http://tonycampolo.org/if-i-had-to-live-it-over-again/#.V1_8-MenPrk

Part 1: Chapter 1 – page 12
Lizzie Velasquez's Story
http://imwithlizzie.com
https://www.youtube.com/watch?v=QzPbY9ufnQY

Part 2: Chapter 5 – page 23
Charles Blondin reference
http://www.notablebiographies.com/supp/Supplement-A-Bu-and-Obituaries/Blondin-Charles.html
http://www.inspire21.com/stories/faithstories/CharlesBlondin

www.ingramcontent.com/pod-product-compliance
Lightning Source LLC
Chambersburg PA
CBHW050530300426
44113CB00012B/2031